Merchants of the Sixteenth Century

Contents

Advisory Editor in the Humanities and Social Sciences: Benjamin Nelson

MERCHANTS OF THE SIXTEENTH CENTURY

English translation copyright © 1972 by Harper & Row.

First HARPER PAPERBACK edition published 1972.

STANDARD BOOK NUMBER: 06-138878-5

LIBRARY OF CONGRESS CATALOG CARD NUMBER: 75-161638

Designed by C. Linda Dingler

Merchants
of the
Sixteenth Century

PIERRE JEANNIN

Translated by Paul Fittingoff

HF
493
J413

HARPER & ROW, PUBLISHERS
New York, Evanston, San Francisco, London

Merchants of the Sixteenth Century

I

The Century of the Fuggers

The sixteenth century cannot be summed up in the definitions of a few terms such as "Renaissance" and "Reformation." Even more inappropriate are those labels in theoretical explanations, which give the impression of a succession of abrupt and sweeping changes. Certainly, in the course of the century everything was transformed; yet history does not proceed by sudden leaps. The acceleration in the circulation of new ideas can also be observed in other fields, compared to which it is clear that its tempo in the field of ideas was rather restrained. The men of this age were pioneering in other realms than that of the mind.

This verbose century, when talk was parlayed into money, was a dynamic period: merchants increased their wealth and enhanced their status. Owing to the rapid growth of the economy, money came to occupy a more important place in the hierarchy of social values, and finance began to play a greater role in the life of the state. An adventurous oligarchy embodied both commercial and political power, and the enterprises launched by the oligarchy were only the most visible manifestations—the history "in the grand manner"—of currents affecting the most fundamental structures of society.

In the immense army of merchants, the biggest businessmen, whose interests were global in scope and whose co-operation was sought by sovereigns, constituted the "general staff." No less important, however, was the industrious infantry, who was engaged in far more modest, but equally constructive, tasks; these obscure "privates" won as many battles as the "generals," although in different ways. It should be pointed out, however, that the "general staff" was also a spearhead and, in this respect, fully deserves the special interest it has received. It was this vanguard that, more than sixty years ago, Richard Ehrenberg chose to examine; his book on the money magnates of the sixteenth century, with its simple but eloquent title, *The Century of the Fuggers*, remains a classic fundamental study. As long ago as 1560, Ludovico Guicciardini, in his famous *Description of All the Low Countries*, noted the pre-eminent position of the Fuggers of Augsburg and described the head of this family as the prince of all merchants in his century. Indeed, their story offers the devotees of biography many an opportunity to sound the epic trumpet, to celebrate their power, and to extol the genius of Jakob the Rich, who established their greatness.

Because of their exceptional position during the first sixty years of the sixteenth century, the Fugger family must be viewed as a unique phenomenon. Certain characteristics were unusually pronounced among the Fuggers, whereas other traits, generally found in the common run of merchants, were barely discernible—the Fuggers do not follow any general pattern. But their wealth, far above the average for this period, was still part of the general trend of increasing prosperity among the entire merchant class. And so, before studying the complex entity in depth, let us draw a few significant, if not wholly typical, examples from the history of the Fugger family.

THE FOUNDER

Up until the time of Jakob the Rich, there was nothing to distinguish the Fuggers from the other merchants of Augsburg. At the very beginning, we find a modest person—a reasonably well-to-do weaver, both an artisan and a tradesman; he died in 1409. His progeny formed into two branches, and one branch, the Fuggers von der Gilgen (so called because of the lilies that appeared in their coat of arms after 1473), would win renown in the sixteenth century. The other branch achieved an enviable degree of prosperity during the fifteenth century; however, until the middle of the 1490s, the "Gilgen" were overshadowed by the "Reh" (roebuck). Lucas Fugger vom Reh, whose family had been among the first in Augsburg to have dealings in Antwerp (around 1480), was awarded the town's most coveted honor. The roebuck Fuggers traded in Italy, and the volume of their business, particularly in Venice and Milan, far exceeded that which Jakob the Elder and his sons, from the Gilgen branch, had achieved when they had started out some years before. This was still no higher than the level frequently attained by the other Augsburg merchants, whose activities included the traditional trade with Italy, the importation of spices, silks, cotton, and saffron, and the export of manufactured textile and metal goods. However, a few rather less routine transactions were already appearing in the offices of the Fuggers: in the statement of bankruptcy of Lucas Fugger vom Reh, mention was made of the loss of 10,000 florins lent to the Emperor, guaranteed by the city of Louvain, which had failed to fulfill its obligations. In the years following Lucas's bankruptcy, his descendants and their relations—some of whom settled in Nuremberg, others in Warsaw —were to emerge as agents for the great Fuggers, the descendants of Jakob the Elder, who had died in 1469.

Two of Jakob's five sons died shortly after him. The youngest son, Jakob the Second, had been destined for the priesthood, but he gave up his clerical career in 1473 and, with his brothers Ulrich and Georg, went into commerce. After serving a few years of apprenticeship in Italy, Jakob began to bring about new departures in his affairs. In that same year—1473—Ulrich, for the first time, lent money to Emperor Frederick III. But it was Jakob who, in 1487, got Siegmund, the Habsburg Duke of Tyrol, to sign a contract that then served as a model for many other contracts designed to guarantee the repayment of large loans: as security Jakob secured a mortgage on the Archduke's share of the silver produced in the Archduke's mines. A few years after gaining a foothold in the Tyrol, the Fuggers employed the same methods to gain entry to

Hungary, where for a time they were partners with the powerful Austrian family of Thurzo.

The exploitation of mines, ironworks, and foundries, the sale of silver, and, even more, of copper, and banking operations were essential ingredients of the Fugger fortune. The Fugger interests extended throughout central Europe and into the Low Countries and Italy. Their business establishment in Rome played a very important role up to 1527, for the church money transferred to the Papal Curia from most of the transalpine regions passed through the hands of the Fuggers. But a few sentences cannot do justice to the myriad activities. One would have to mention their twenty separate mining operations, the jewelry and luxurious fabrics they provided to various courts, and their participation in the financing of the Portuguese spice trade. Occasionally, they would take charge of minting ateliers, as they did in Rome during the papacies of Julius II and Leo X. From 1530 on, they were also manufacturing large quantities of fustian, a mixed cotton which was woven on their extensive estates in the Ulm region and sold on the Netherlands and Italian markets.

The guiding spirit in these diverse enterprises was that of Jakob alone; he had fought tooth and nail to gain equality with his older brothers, and his leadership was already evident in the partnership agreement that the three signed in 1494—the first formal "joint-stock" agreement. The partnership's name would change several times: "Ulrich Fugger and his Brothers," "Jakob Fugger and his Nephews," "Anton Fugger and his Nephews," "Marx Fugger and his Brothers." Despite all these changes two basic policies would remain untouched. First, female offspring were excluded from the partnership and were simply given a sum of money for their dowry; only males were allowed to own shares, though a few men were also excluded, on grounds of incompetence: Hieronymus (1499–1538), for example, was dismissed by his uncle. Secondly, the firm was always to be led by one man, rather than by a board of directors: thus, when Jakob died childless, in 1525, his nephew Anton took over. As fate would have it, a number of premature deaths occurred in the family. This meant that (before 1560, at any rate) there were never more than two or three persons qualified to run the business—a circumstance which made for more effective leadership.

Thus, between 1495 and 1525, thanks to the entrepreneurial skill of Jakob the Rich, particularly in his capacity as chief financier for the Habsburgs, the Fuggers established themselves as the largest commercial and banking firm in all Europe. Jakob's involvement in the election of Charles V to the imperial crown in 1519 was decisive: of the 850,000 florins needed to purchase the votes of the Electors, the Fuggers furnished more than 540,000. Shortly before, the agents of the Fuggers had been collecting the payments for indulgences, the levying of which provoked the Lutheran revolt; half of the amount went into the Fuggers' coffers as repayment for a loan made to Albert of Brandenburg when he bought the archbishopric of Mainz. An image of the big banker with both halves of the world—the Pope and the Emperor—tied to his purse strings is hardly an exaggeration. In the words of an Augsburg chronicler, whose acounts have been shown to be accurate: "The names of Jakob Fugger and his nephews were known in every kingdom and every region, even amongst the heathens. Emperors, kings, princes, and lords sent emissaries to him; the Pope hailed him and embraced him as his own dear son; the cardinals stood up when he appeared. All the merchants in the world called him an inspired man, and he amazed the heathens." Jakob's life reads more like a legend than a true story.

The power he accumulated in a mere quarter of a century seems so great that it is tempting to regard his ascent as a smooth and easy process, and overlook the fierce battles he waged against competitors. Such battles occurred, for example, over control of the copper market, and with certain governments, both municipalities and states, in order to protect his lines of communication, which covered almost the entire continent. With the Habsburgs—perpetual borrowers who were rarely in a position to pay off their debts—he found it necessary to act with caution. He would grant them no credits unless they, in return, granted him special privileges, protection, or solid guarantees, such as assigning income to him or pledging certain very tangible possessions—landed property in many cases, sometimes the crown jewels, and so forth. In these operations there was a need for both flexibility and considerable firmness. Gifts great or small were judiciously given to preserve useful friendships. Moreover, it was often necessary to mobilize the enterprise of learned men—for example, the humanist Dr. Conrad Peutinger, town clerk of Augsburg—to help him when conflicts arose. Running such a business was no easier than governing a country.

DECLINE OF A MERCHANT DYNASTY

Jakob the Rich successfully overcame all the obstacles in his path. But just at the time of his death, the Fuggers were caught in a fierce storm in Hungary: *jacqueries*, a sudden epidemic of xenophobia among the nobility—everything was going against them. Anton needed as much patience as diplomacy to set things right in this vital sector; and he was able to do this by taking advantage of the Habsburgs' acquisition of the Hungarian crown, the crown of St. Stephen.

In 1527, the Fugger trading office in Rome was liquidated, but on the whole, the leader of the second generation tenaciously held onto the properties he had inherited. Certain operations, indeed, became more profitable than ever before, and the volume of his financial transactions with the Emperor and with the King of England reached fantastic proportions. One result of this was to shift the company's center of gravity toward the west, to Antwerp and Spain. This development was fraught with dangers which, in the long run, would prove more serious than any temporary setback, however severe. In 1546, the Fuggers' assets reached a record level, but the burden of their Spanish operations, where large amounts of capital were frozen in imperial undertakings, was growing heavier and heavier. There were certain risks in becoming Charles V's principal creditor. Anton Fugger faithfully lent his support to the war efforts against France and against the German Protestants, and at first, his profits from these ventures were considerable, since the

Fugger story, however, contains two significant variations. On occasion, their wealth would be squandered, with bankruptcy the result; at other times, members of the family acceded to the nobility. The legal acquisition of titles and noble prerogatives, however, did not always signify a break with the past. In 1507, Jakob the Rich purchased from Maximilian the counties of Kirchberg and Weissenhorn and several other estates together with the various rights that went with them. All of this was simply incorporated into the landed property belonging to the firm. Jakob, now a count and the suzerain of numerous subjects, seemed less taken with the prestige of the title than with the soundness of the investment; he had no thought of living in the noble manner. Similarly, Anton and his brother did not appear at all eager to flaunt the titles the Emperor had bestowed on them in 1530. On the other hand, their descendants, by degrees, became noblemen in temperament. Even those who remained in commerce, far from wanting to run everything themselves, were content merely to watch over the firm's operations from on high. Thus, the financiers ultimately became the progenitors of a family of nobles, although, in the case of the Fuggers, the transformation proceeded more slowly than in many other, less wealthy families.

Wealth's power to transform is evident in the history of the Fuggers. Before his marriage in 1498, Jakob the Rich spent little on his own person; afterwards, his style of living became ostentatious. Many a princess might have envied his wife's finery and jewels. The receptions he gave in his spacious home (one of several houses he owned in Augsburg) to honor illustrious guests, were incomparable in their splendor. For him, such extravagance was almost always connected with some important business deal. He was not indifferent to considerations of prestige. His gifts to churches were motivated as much by the desire to display his munificence as by piety. When the older Fuggers had had a chapel or altar erected or a stained-glass window designed, they were never close-fisted. They called on the finest workmen, always. But at the same time, they insisted on having their coat of arms emblazoned on every work. These benefactors did not seek anonymity; rather, they felt that their gifts should enhance the glory of their family name, as well as promote the salvation of their souls. For the deserving poor of Augsburg, Jakob the Rich founded not a traditional almshouse, but a miniature city within the city: the famous *Fuggerei*, which consisted of 106 independent dwellings. Occupancy, however, was not given as alms to the poor—a symbolic rent was charged. Thus, medieval charity was turning into social paternalism. The clergy were assigned no role at all in this institution, although the fortunate inmates were obliged to recite, each day, a *Pater*, an *Ave*, and a *Credo* for the souls of the founders and their family.

One cannot deny that the religious sentiment that inspired these acts of charity, and that, moreover, prompted the Fuggers to insert in their wills detailed dispositions regarding the masses and other rites to be celebrated after their death, was truly profound. But this religiosity had very little, if anything, to do with intellectual disquietude. Nothing is known of Jakob's studies (if indeed he studied at all) during that brief period in his youth when he was preparing for the priesthood; he apparently never showed any interest in speculative knowledge. He did employ artists—*fortune oblige*—but, unlike several grand-nephews or even Anton, for that matter, he was not a real Maecenas or humanist. His life was geared for action; there was no place in it for art or culture. When someone suggested to Jakob that, in view of certain difficulties, it might be best to wind up his commercial activities in Hungary, his reply was unequivocal: "I want to make as much money as I can." When we come to Anton, we find that the lines are not drawn so sharply; with age, wealth grew less brutal and acquired a kind of urbanity. But had it not been for the implacable drive of the founding father, it is unlikely that any of his heirs could have become erudite collectors of antique objects and works of art. (With this change, those heirs, although still of interest to the historian, ceased to hold any fascination for their contemporaries.) The name of Fugger became a common noun in the sixteenth century, synonymous with big businessman—*Fucker* in Lübeck, *Fokker* in Antwerp, *fouckeur* in Wallonia, *fucar* in Spain; and, because of its resemblance to the German word for usury, certain derogatory expressions were derived from it *(Fugger, Wucher, fuggerisch, wucherisch)*. The privilege of becoming a "type" in the popular imagination, despite the disadvantages of such notoriety, might have been a great source of personal pride to Jakob Fugger, who once declared himself "rich by the grace of God."

May we not consider this proud affirmation of the legitimate power of money an indication that the world had changed and that men had recognized this fact? Was this, perhaps, the birth of modern capitalism? But, before the Fuggers, there had been the Medici—and they had not been the first, either. It is not my intention to review all the arguments, pro and con, concerning the "modernity" of the sixteenth century—a subject that has been rather thoroughly explored. But, in this connection, mention must be made of recent additions to our knowledge of the Italian businessmen of the Middle Ages, particularly the scope of their enterprises, the refinement of their techniques, and their pre-eminent role in social and cultural evolution.

Moreover, capitalism is not simply a matter of temperament or individual success. Limiting ourselves to a few very broad generalizations, we see that social and economic structures in the sixteenth century were still far more feudal than capitalistic. Since the technical bases for large-scale production were completely lacking, subsistence agriculture was—and would remain, for some time to come—the primary form of economic activity. Almost everywhere, supply (at the level of production) and demand (at the level of consumption) were measured in small, widely scattered units. Concentration occurred fairly frequently and to a significant degree only in the area of foreign travel. There was thus a commercial and financial capitalism, quite distinct from the industrial capitalism of the nineteenth century.

Of course, during the sixteenth century, some merchants did increase their control of certain branches of manufacturing and, by that fact, could be called "industrialists." (The Fuggers, as we have seen, were in this category.) We must also take into account those noblemen and churchmen who engaged in business, although, as a rule this was not their vocation. But commerce, pure and simple, must be our starting point. In order to see what was involved in the "conduct of merchandising," we must observe the merchant in his shop or office, follow him in his travels, and look through his account books and his correspondence. In order to understand his methods of work, the sources of his profits, and the risks he had to take—in the hope of eventually gaining some insight into his social behavior and his mentality—it is necessary to describe the "medium" in which he operated. In other words, before limning the physiognomy of the merchant, we must examine the physiology of commerce.

II

The World of the Merchants

The European businessman's field of action extended far beyond Europe; for explorers, whose voyages had been financed, in large part, by the businessman himself, had pushed back the boundaries of the unknown, to the west and to the east. A complete economic tableau should include not only Europe, but also her overseas extensions, where conditions varied considerably. Black Africa and America—with their primitive inhabitants who, where necessary, had been reduced to total submission—were virtually virgin territory for the traders. On the other hand, in the East Indies, as in the Muslim world (with which they were already quite familiar), it was necessary to deal with the local merchants, a highly developed and powerful class. But whether in a shop or an outpost of empire, the activities of Europeans overseas were always conditioned by the interests of their own particular country, city, or company. They employed the same techniques customarily used in Europe, with very few modifications; between their civilization and that of their Arab, Hindu, or Chinese clients and suppliers, there was a sharp divide. Therefore, this study is limited.

Europe can be viewed as a complex consisting of three distinct maritime regions and a central sector (whose function, it should be noted, was not limited to linking together the three coastal hinterlands).

The Mediterranean is Europe's gateway to the Near East, which was the main focus of the flourishing commerce of the Middle Ages. From the depths of the colder lands to the north, across the Baltic Sea, came products that, though less exotic than those of the Orient, were just as much in demand in the west European market. From the Straits of Denmark to Gibraltar, the Atlantic and her extensions had been the highway connecting economically advanced regions engaged in vigorous trading—long before her waters were to bear the hopes and ordeals of the conquerors of new worlds. Between these maritime zones, with links to all three, and, at different times, enjoying a special relationship with each of them, lay central Europe, stretching from Lyons and the Rhine region to the edge of the Russian steppe, traversed by a system of highways and waterways, and criss-crossed by a network of trading towns no less prosperous than the seaports. This schema should serve our purpose, provided we allow it a certain flexibility.

MEDITERRANEAN COMMERCE

The oldest sea in our history—its very name still evokes memories of ancient Rome—was for Europe (whose maritime predominance had been challenged by the Arabs and the Turks) the only practicable route to the treasures of the Orient—at least until the Portuguese discovered the passage round the Cape. And, of course, one cannot say "Mediterranean" without at once thinking "Italy."

Trade with the Levant was based primarily on silks and spices. But many other commodities—salt, wheat, wines, and oil—also circulated around the inland sea. In normal times, these products were of minor importance in the world of trade, but in the case of certain basic foodstuffs, "normalcy" was exceptional. Since grain harvests often fell short of requirements—such disasters were not confined to the lands bordering on the Mediterranean nor to the sixteenth century—grain had to be imported. But the grain traffic, as a rule, remained essentially interregional in character until the end of the century or thereabouts, and for the most part consisted of small operations conducted by petty traders. The regular traffic was of an entirely different character, involving the mobilization of large quantities of capital, which brought Europe exotic merchandise purchased in Egypt and Syria. Numerous agents, residing more or less permanently in the principal market cities (Alexandria, Cairo, Beirut, Damascus), had the goods loaded onto large galleys bound for the West. The suppliers were Arab merchants, who imported East Indian products by way of the Red Sea or the Persian Gulf. Spices made up the bulk of these imports; but there are spices and there are spices. Pepper, which was relatively common, heavy, and inexpensive, was not handled in the same way as cinnamon, cloves, or nutmeg.

No less important was silk, the raw material for an industry of which the Italians were the undisputed masters. Exporting the dazzling luxuries of their Renaissance proved to be a good stroke of business, for it opened up new markets for them. More humble commodities made up the remainder of the cargoes from the Orient: cotton (which was still considered a third-rate fabric), rice, and sugar (though, by this time, the Atlantic islands had become the principal sugar producers). It would be almost impossible to enumerate all the products traded, and in any case, such a list is hardly necessary for our purposes. We should, however, examine the traffic moving in the opposite direction. To the Levant went cloth (from Italy, Languedoc, and distant points in northwestern Europe), an indescribable assortment of small items ("notions") turned out by the industries of the West, and, later on, grain, salt, saffron, and timber. But the total value of Europe's exports was nowhere near that of her imports.

Commerce with the Orient consumed enormous quantities of precious metal. Gold was already in short supply by the end of the fifteenth century, since the output of the Sudan, the western part of which was in Portuguese hands, was no longer reaching the Maghreb, where it could be picked up by the Italians. Silver, on the other hand, was being produced in ever greater abundance in the mines of central Europe. Italy's dealings with the transalpine regions to the north and west were bound up with her operations in the Near East and represented another important source of wealth. West of Genoa, there were no major trading towns on the Mediterranean seaboard. Neither Barcelona nor Valencia nor Marseilles played a role, at the international level, comparable to that of Ragusa (Dubrovnik), that remarkable city where several Balkan trade routes converged. In Italy proper, there were few cities that did not produce a famous dynasty or two for the world of international commerce. Among her largest trading towns were Genoa, Florence, Milan, and Venice—to name only a few.

Venice, in the words of Fernand Braudel, "battened on the excess fat of the Turkish Empire." From the heart of this city of waterways, the Doges commanded an unrivaled constellation of fleets and a unique network of first-rate correspondents. Venice was also a great clearing-house for trade "bulletins" from the Orient. Her hinterland stretches across the Alps into upper Germany, for which she was, in certain respects, a bridgehead on the Mediterranean. The city welcomed visiting Germans but kept a close watch on them; they were confined to the famous Fondaco dei Tedeschi, a combination hotel, warehouse, and market. Meanwhile, the other city–states maintained close relations with Nuremberg and Augsburg, stops on the road to the north. To the west, there were more direct routes to the Low Countries—either through Lyons and the Rhineland, or around the Iberian Peninsula by galley. Italian merchants traveled all these routes, and kept western Europe supplied with the products of their own industries, and with fruit from the Mediterranean region and spices from the Levant. Italy also exported alum, an important raw material in the manufacture of cloth. Renaissance Italy, having accumulated much experience and much capital, with trading colonies that in many cases dominated the host countries' largest market towns, remained in the forefront of European commerce.

BALTIC COMMERCE

The Baltic Sea was the Mediterranean of the North, and the symmetry was, up to a point, economic as well as geographic. Here too, there was a large market for cloth manufactured in the West; here too, large quantities of silver changed hands. The commerical position of the Hanseatic League corresponded to that of the Italians; Lübeck was the northern counterpart of Venice. But behind these similarities, there were many striking differences. First, a difference in age: in the North, urban economies with large "spheres of influence" were not much in evidence before the thirteenth century, whereas in the Roman world, the large towns had been a very important factor from earliest times. The unappealing lands around the Baltic, where the winters were extremely harsh, were thinly populated; they were, in every respect, underdeveloped areas.

The specific characteristics of Baltic commerce can be traced to these conditions. The Baltic region regularly supplied western and central Europe with an abundance of unprocessed materials: wood, potash, pitch, and tar. Striking proof of the primitive character of the region's economy is the fact that among the items it produced for exchange were furs, for the adornment of luxurious garments as well as for comfort, and wax, for the candles of the pious. Although livestock breeding and agriculture produced mediocre yields, sizable quantities of grain, flax, hemp, wool, hides, and animal fats were exported on a regular basis. If we add iron and copper from Sweden and salted or dried fish from the fisheries of Norway and Sweden, we shall have a complete list of the staple commodities of Baltic commerce. The preparation of both fish and hides required large amounts of salt; ocean salt from the Atlantic coast, together with cloth, made up the bulk of the region's imports. Other imports included wines, spices, metal products, glass, and paper. From the standpoint of its commercial structure, the North still resembled a newly settled territory.

In the fourteenth century, all Baltic trade was in the hands of the Hanseatic merchants. However, the unity of their "empire"—based on their unique methods of work, similar institutions, and a common language (Middle Low German)—was starting to crack, allowing the English and the Netherlanders to slip in. But at the beginning of the sixteenth century, these new factors did not yet seriously affect the commercial position of the Hanseatic traders, who regularly served as intermediaries between the West and the vast lands of the Northeast. Lübeck was still at the center of a web that reached to Novgorod, Bruges, London, Cologne, and across the sea to Stockholm and Bergen. Together with Hamburg, she had launched and then actively promoted the development of the cities to the east. She was not the capital, but rather the pilot city, of the Hanseatic League, whose leading merchants were still in the habit of dealing with sovereigns on an equal footing.

However, since the fifteenth century, the system's equilibrium had been threatened by the rise of the cities of the eastern Baltic, which more and more were dealing directly—by way of the Sund—with the cities on the North Sea. But those new detours and short cuts did not break the chain of interests in which Lübeck was the central and essential link.

CENTRAL EUROPE

Since the fourteenth century, the cities of southern Germany, inside the angle formed by the Rhine and the Danube, had experienced very rapid economic growth. Nuremberg had led the way—hence, her dominant role in German culture of the fifteenth and sixteenth centuries—but Augsburg was not far behind. The whole region surrounding these two great centers pulsated with commercial and industrial activity. Commodities were brought in from Italy and shipped to the northwestern, northern, and eastern parts of Europe; high-quality textile and metal goods were produced for export. By 1500, the Grosse Gesellschaft of Ravensburg had an agency or branch office in Bern and Geneva, Lyons,

Avignon, and Marseilles, Milan and Genoa, Barcelona, Valencia, and Saragossa, Antwerp, Cologne, and Nuremberg, Vienna and Budapest. If we look at the situation in its entirety, central European trade appears as one of the factors in the German thrust to the east, the slowing down of which was already having political repercussions. The Germans maintained trading colonies in Poland, Bohemia, and Hungary. If the Turkish presence in the southeast constituted a barrier, not easily crossed, the roads passing to the north of the Carpathians were as heavily traveled as ever. The products of Poland and Russia reached southern Germany by this route, while Germans and Italians followed these roads to Cracow and beyond, sometimes establishing contacts with the Baltic markets. Their activities in the cities of Poland complemented those of the local bourgeoisie; moreover, toward the southeast—in Lublin and Lvov —they established connections with traders from Greece and Armenia —a part of the Orient they hardly knew.

Meanwhile, Nuremberg and Augsburg, in addition to their trade with the east, were discovering business opportunities in the west as well: in Frankfurt, Cologne, and Antwerp. A great highway called the Hohe Landstrasse led from Frankfurt to Erfurt (which owed its wealth to the pastel of Thuringia) and from there to Leipzig (which since the fifteenth century had been a rallying point to which many merchants had migrated).

Throughout the continent, the same general conditions prevailed regarding the movement of goods. Grain was rarely shipped over long distances. The wagon was the most common means of overland transport, and higher-priced commodities that took up less space were the most actively traded; these included wines, fabrics, spices, wax, furs, and leather goods. Bulkier items were more easily transported along the waterways. Almost everywhere, the largest transactions took place in the metal trade and the mining and metallurgical industries.

Metallurgical industries, drawing on rather meager but easily accessible ore deposits, had sprung up all over Europe during the Middle Ages, and become distinctive features of certain regional economies. (Besides metals, the subsoil contained other riches of considerable interest to businessmen—alum, among others, and the minerals of the salt marshes.) When the metallurgical industries expanded, central Europe held its own, creating enterprises organized along entirely new lines. In this connection, we have extended the boundaries of central Europe to include the ironworks of Liège, and the copper industry that brought wealth and fame to Dinant and Aix-la-Chapelle. Outside this perimeter, there were very few mines—except in Sweden and the British Isles—with yields much in excess of local needs.

As mining techniques improved, central Europe began extracting a variety of ores, some more valuable than others: small amounts of zinc and lead, much copper. Moreover, every seam contained some silver. This region remained, until the middle of the century, the principal source of the white metal, for which the European economy was always starving, it seems. This was certainly the most compelling reason for the rise of the German merchants who owned these mines to a leading position in the international business community. But their profits did not come from silver alone; copper and iron were also in continuous demand because of the steady growth of the arms industry. Copper was also being used more and more in the coining of money, but the copper producers' most profitable outlet was the colonial trade; the Portuguese, for example, exported enormous quantities of the metal to Africa and the Indies—in the form of baubles and trinkets. This particular illustration shows clearly which way trade was moving at the dawn of the sixteenth century: not only were the leading firms of southern Germany conducting more and more business in Antwerp, but continental trade as a whole—because of the upsurge of the Atlantic economy—was being pulled in this direction.

THE ATLANTIC SEABOARD

Around the year 1500, Europe, north and south, presented symptoms that appear contradictory at first glance. Venice was in agony, Augsburg was triumphant: both conditions reflected the new conjuncture resulting from the opening of the transoceanic routes. The focal points of world trade were shifting toward the Atlantic, toward Lisbon, Antwerp, and Seville. The effects of this change on the older centers of trade were dramatic, at least initially. But economic developments are too complex to be reduced to a single chain of events with neat divisions representing the decline of one city and the rise of another. The history of the discoveries themselves is a perfect illustration of the law that states that the most brilliant successes—the epoch-making events—are the work of many unknown hands and are years in the preparation. There is no other way to explain the sudden expansion of Portugal and Castile. This was the first important manifestation of the dynamic forces agitating all of western Europe, from the Iberian Peninsula to the Low Countries and the British Isles. Every branch of industry was clearly experiencing an accelerated turnover—from the French and Iberian salt trade to wine production in every vineyard from Andalusia to the Rhineland, from the export of Castilian wool and Toulouse pastel to the expansion of textile manufacturing (which had, in part, been transformed). In the latter industry, England took the lead with her *ostades* and *carisés,* while the Low Countries were busy turning out lightweight fabrics, and the whole western part of France was actively engaged in the production of linen. These successes, though perhaps not so sensational, are certainly as interesting as those of the Iberian explorers in the Atlantic.

Having established bases in Morocco, Madeira, and the Azores in the fifteenth century, the Portuguese—in their quest for gold, ivory, and slaves—continued to move down the coast of Africa; this undertaking culminated in the voyage (in 1497) of Vasco da Gama, who sailed all the way to Calcutta. (Christopher Columbus had already been back in Seville for six years.) Commercially, the first area to be affected by these discoveries was the spice market, in which, for the next half-century or so, Venice and the Levant would be relegated to a minor position. The flow of precious metals from the Americas to Spain had far-reaching and lasting consequences; the sudden increase in the supply of these metals had an immediate and profound impact on prices and the volume of business. Lord Malestroit was not the first to observe (in 1566) that "strange it is that all things are becoming dearer nowadays, so much that each and every one of us, whether great or humble, must feel it in his purse."

The establishment of the Portuguese spice trade at Antwerp was the final stage of a movement which had been steadily drawing merchants and merchandise to the banks of the Scheldt. Only now did the term "world market" acquire its full significance. Antwerp brought North and South together; people came here from Danzig and Leipzig, from Venice, Lisbon, and London. "The commerce and trading of all these merchants, be they foreigners or natives of the country, is beyond belief and wonderful to behold, as much for the number of exchanges as for the quantities of goods in the warehouses." Thus remarked Ludovico Guicciardini, an excellent observer, whose writings, moreover, abound with such expressions of wonderment. It was the combination of English cloth, South German metals, and colonial products that was mainly responsible for Antwerp's prodigious growth. This city alone handled more than three-fourths of the Low Countries' trade.

Practically every commercial firm engaged in international trade had a branch office or a licensed correspondent in Antwerp. But there was also a multitude of smaller firms here. The largest business operations were conducted by Italians, Spaniards, Portuguese, South Germans, and natives of Antwerp; with the exception of the English, who, through their "companies of merchant adventurers," secured a monopoly on cloth exports to the region between the Somme and Emden.

The Kings of Spain and Portugal organized their colonial trade on a monopolistic basis, and, in principle, foreigners were excluded. Everything had to go through the Casa de la Contratación in Seville or the Casa da India in Lisbon (where the King had become a spice merchant). But neither Spain nor Portugal could do without the services and the capital which only the large, international firms could supply. Thus, the treasures from overseas eventually reached Antwerp. The city's deep involvement in the East Indian and West Indian trade acted as a stimulus to her whole economy, commercial and industrial.

But contemporaries were even more impressed by another feature of the Antwerp scene. With gold and silver pouring into the city, the money market was expanding rapidly. In fact, the volume and frequency of financial transactions were so great that an inexperienced observer might fail to see that the traffic in money had not eclipsed the commodities market and that there had really been no significant innovations in its mechanisms or techniques. The famous Bourse, erected in 1531, where merchants, "for one hour, converse, discussing in particular deposits and exchanges," was merely a continuation of those meetings of exchange brokers held in Bruges a century before. But with the tremendous increase in public loans, the field of finance, in which the Italian bankers had long been past masters and in which the Germans had been engaged since the fifteenth century, now offered limitless possibilities.

In 1551, the Consulat, that is, the municipality of Lyons, vaunted "the great concourse of the richest foreign merchants who come each year to our fair from all parts of Christendom, even from Cairo, Constantinople, and Greece, in order to contract, one with the other, for merchandise and monetary exchanges." Lyons was, for the Kingdom of France, the main door to Italy and the Orient; and, since it was the closest trading town to south Germany, it served as a rendezvous point for businessmen from this area and Mediterranean Spain. The Italians played a prominent part at Lyons.

Lyons's influence extended to all of France (both the inland and coastal regions), the Low Countries, and England. However, so long as she was a great trading town (Lyons's rise and fall coincided almost exactly with Antwerp's), her main activities were connected with the older central European and Mediterranean trade along the roads to the east and south. But both cities were destined to be left behind as the international situation evolved.

THE FRUITS OF EXPANSION

A rather widely accepted interpretation of the sixteenth century emphasizes the contrast between the prosperity of the first half (which, came to an end around 1540 or 1550, according to this view) and the troubles and hardships of the following period: monetary crises, grave financial problems, political and religious disorders in France and the Low Countries, the increasing perils of sea travel. However, the indices of economic activity—which are, admittedly, quite rudimentary owing to the dearth of statistical information for this century—suggest a different pattern. By studying the movement of certain key commodities and, especially, the fluctuations in prices—which, over the long run, tended to rise—we can perceive a trend toward expansion which first manifested itself before 1500 and lasted until after 1600.

There were periods when business seemed on the verge of collapse—these occurred at intervals of approximately thirty years, around 1530, 1555, and 1600—but the basic tendency was never reversed. What characterized this century, overshadowing all its vicissitudes, was its dynamism: whenever an artery of commerce appeared to be drying up, a replacement for it was found immediately, and even those regions that were hardest hit were able to launch new enterprises. Venice, for example, ousted from the spice trade at the beginning of the sixteenth century, got her second wind after a few decades. Shipments of spices began to make their way through the Persian Gulf to the ports of the eastern Mediterranean. The Venetians themselves energetically set about building up their cloth industry. The South Germans, meanwhile, had a finger in every pie; though Antwerp was now in the ascendancy, the great commercial houses of Augsburg and Nuremberg showed no inclination to give up the Fondaco dei Tedeschi.

The concentration of economic power in the Low Countries stimulated the development of seaports, like Riga and especially Danzig, which were outlets for regions dependent on massive exports. But the Low Countries' closest neighbors were the ones who clearly benefited most from the economic boom in Antwerp and the Iberian Peninsula. To the north, for instance, French merchants began to penetrate the Baltic region. The advances made by English commerce were most remarkable, in every area from Russia to the south seas.

The oceanic highways attracted daring men who found adventure not only in trading, but also in privateering or fishing at the Grand Banks off Newfoundland. These highways were jealously guarded by the Spanish and the Portuguese, but this did not prevent the English from reaching Labrador, nor Rouen merchants from traveling as far as Brazil and even Sumatra. These expeditions did not lead to the establishment of regular runs; there was still smuggling and the plundering of ships returning from the Indies, as well as more respectable commercial activities in Lisbon, Seville, the islands, and along the African coast. The Iberian Peninsula, together with its extensions in the East and West Indies, offered an enormous consumer market. Advancing southward, traders from the regions bordering on the English Channel and the North Sea passed through the Straits of Gibraltar and eventually reached the Levant. Starting in the earlier half of the century, they had reconnoitered these unfamiliar places one after the other, tested them, and sometimes abandoned them temporarily.

The tremendous concentration of trading activity in the Antwerp market generated the rapid growth, paralleling or complementing that of Antwerp, of other mercantile cities. When this market began to break up in 1570, trade shifted to other towns, and new lines of communication were set up. When widespread privateering by the Protestant countries prevented silver convoys from sailing directly to the Low Countries, an alternative route was organized: Barcelona–Genoa–Milan–Frankfurt–Antwerp. Similarly, shipments of Spanish wool, also subject to harassment in northern waters, were frequently re-routed through Italy. Generally speaking, Italian trade (the Genoese business community especially) was revitalized during this period. Not long after, Leghorn, in its turn, entered an era of great prosperity. In the long-term view, however, a decisive shift was taking place in the distribution of power, and the chief beneficiaries were the commercial powers of the north. The great conflict between Philip II and the Protestant world was an occasion for much rejoicing in Rouen, a neutral junction, which was becoming a great international trading center; and things were much the same elsewhere. The Hanseatic League's Iberian trade went through an extraordinary boom. And Marseilles's trade with the Levant, which had been crawling along for fifty years, suddenly soared, thanks to her neutrality in the Holy League's war against the Turks.

Toward the end of the sixteenth century, the Dutch, who had cut their eyeteeth in enterprises that were sometimes humble and unproductive, established their primacy. They grew fat on the substance of the Spanish Empire, which fought them yet could not do without them. Before long they would undertake the conquest of the Portuguese Empire; they would come to rule the seas and make Amsterdam the chief market for the precious metals and every important commodity. Other northern cities—Hamburg, Danzig, and especially London—were borne along by the same tide, though this did not prevent mercantile conflicts from erupting within the Protestant world itself. But the rise of the North, with the concomitant shift in Europe's balance of power, was largely dependent on the continuing vitality of the major arteries of the Spanish–American economy; the volume of trade between Seville and America did not reach its high point until 1606–1610. In the long run, the development of new economic structures would have a baneful effect on Italy and the whole Mediterranean world, but this region was not yet showing any signs of paralysis. In Spain, in France, in Germany, during the early years of the seventeenth century, the activity of Italian businessmen attested to the fact that the time was not yet at hand for their withdrawal from the scene—when their decline would prove the necessary condition for others' success. After the economic annexation of the colonial territories, commercial exchanges between the various regions of Europe increased in scope and intensity. The sixteenth century witnessed the establishment and vigorous expansion of a true world market.

III

The Small Tradespeople

The business world of the sixteenth century cannot be reduced to a handful of extraordinary personalities or to those few individuals and families who amassed colossal fortunes. Behind the enormous streams, by contemporary standards, of merchandise and masses of bullion—behind this rapidly circulating, ever-increasing wealth, there were also ordinary people leading rather uneventful lives. The merchant from Rouen whom we observe purchasing three sacks of wool in Antwerp, or the Genoese picking up six cases of sugar in Marseilles—can we simply ignore such people on the grounds that they lack significance? Certainly not, if our primary concern is—as Lucien Febvre insisted—not (or not merely) the "exceptional successes of a few," but rather "the collective effort—the powerful, manifold effort —of an entire class."

It is necessary to distinguish between the "great" and the "small," but one should not imagine that these clear-cut, neatly labeled categories tell the whole story; there were, in fact, numerous gradations between the two. In today's societies, our knowledge of which is constantly being augmented by a proliferation of statistics, this method of classification poses difficult problems for the sociologists who attempt it. All the more so with the sixteenth century. Even if we can make a fair estimate of the turnover of this or that merchant, we must still determine the frequency of the phenomenon represented by this one sample, if our purpose is to depict an entire social group.

For the sake of argument, let us accept as valid the reconstruction, on the basis of tax records, of the hierarchy of incomes in a given city —which is what J. Strieder attempted for Augsburg. He drew up a list of the 143 citizens who paid the highest taxes there. In first place was Sigmund Gossembrot, who was probably worth somewhere between 43,000 and 86,000 florins, that is, almost twenty times as much as the individuals at the bottom of the list (who, however, were still considered rich men). A disparity of this magnitude obviously reflects two distinct levels of wealth; it does not necessarily indicate two different types of merchant. Where should we draw the dividing line? And should it not also be pointed out that to compare this scale with those of other trading towns, with a view to constructing a more generally valid schema, would pose some extremely difficult problems?

In a word, there are other, indispensable criteria, which are a combination of quantitative indices and qualitative evaluations. Such are: total turnover (which can only be estimated), geographical extent of a firm's field of action, the density of its network of factors, or agents and correspondents, and the techniques and scale of its operations. In this light, the outlines of the various categories tend to blur. There was no more common métier than that of merchant in those days. There were merchant-bankers and merchant-laborers and merchant-clothdealers. It is not likely that these perfectly distinct types could be confused, but what of the intermediate categories? Bankers were almost always involved in merchandising; on the other hand, a good many big merchants, who used the letter of exchange as a means of payment, did not take part in large-scale financial operations. Thus, we can define one particular level of large-scale merchandising and one particular branch of banking; such definitions are convenient, if nothing else. Determining a company's field of action also gives rise to some confusion. The fact that a merchant made sales or purchases hundreds of miles away from his homeland does not necessarily mean that he was in the same class with the Fuggers or Grimaldis. To illustrate this point: in 1526, a native of Gotland, together with a Netherlander, formed a company in Antwerp with capital assets of 400 florins; despite his modest standing, he was nonetheless a citizen of the world of international commerce. And how many Bretons would provide similar examples!

Even the dichotomy of wholesale and retail is, in part, factitious. The largest firms never passed up the chance to make even a small profit. For example, Lorenzo and Pietro Capponi's bank in Lyons, a first-class establishment (Lorenzo, in fact, was a Consul of the Florentine nation), exported hats to Venice. Even more typical is the following: in 1562, Christophe Pruynen, treasurer of the city of Antwerp, a relative and business associate of the Schetz family (a famous name in Antwerp finance and commerce), sent a shipload of silks to Stockholm. His factor, whenever possible, sold wholesale to the King and his court; but also recorded in his day-book are several sales involving no more than a few yards of fabric—transactions worthy of a small shopkeeper. There was, of course, a linguistic—and even a legal—distinction between shopkeeping and trade: *institor* versus *mercator*. But, then, how should we classify the retailer (or *Krämer* or haberdasher, if you will) in Leipzig who received, in one shipment, 1400 florins' worth of divers and sundry articles (the supplier was the Grosse Gesellschaft of Ravensburg). A transaction this large would have been a sizeable sale for many merchants engaging in long-distance trading. In a word, the world of merchandising was a complex edifice, the lower levels of which should be thoroughly explored.

From the social point of view, most retail trading took place on the margin of the business world, properly so-called. Consumers made their purchases at the market or in the shops. These two social milieus—two areas of contact between the merchants, on the one hand, and the peasants and artisans, on the other—were the starting points for many illustrious careers in merchandising. In appearance, there is nothing simpler than the idea of a market. Once, or perhaps several times a week, frequently within the confines of a particular plot of ground and a fixed timetable, the inhabitants of the town were offered the widest variety of consumer goods, especially foodstuffs, brought in by the peasants from the surrounding areas: butter and poultry and other secondary products, but especially grain. Because of its role in provisioning the entire population, the market became the hub of urban life; this explains why it was under the constant surveillance of the authorities and was covered by a mass of ordinances and regulations. But the market also had a specifically commercial aspect, namely, the specialized markets, where one could buy wholesale. The legal texts of this period—objects of extensive and very careful research—clearly reveal the antagonisms resulting from the dual character of the market: consumers against exporters, local merchants against itinerant merchants. But on the whole, our information about the social and economic realities behind all the juridical prescriptions and restrictions is still very meager. Specifically, we do not know what significance to attach to purchases made by merchants in their own homes or before the products—grain, for example—reached the market (in principle, such purchases brought severe penalties). In other words, how important was the conflict between the market trade and the traffic outside the market, between the town's traditional policies regarding provisioning and large-scale commercial activities? And, finally, what were the social implications of this problem?

THE RURAL MERCHANT

In certain respects, all this is related to the problem of the rural merchants, who were intermediate between the tillers of the soil and interregional or international commercial enterprises. There is no doubt that this group played an extremely important role in sixteenth-century society, and it cannot be ignored. In many countries, the rural merchants were very much like those merchants from Poitou whose way of life P. Raveau has skillfully reconstructed on the basis of notarial records. Generally, they were dealers in agricultural products, but some were specialists, combining trade with the processing of raw materials. In this category were the merchant-tanners, who were often related to, or in league with, the merchant-butchers; they dealt in tallow or wool, and their livelihood was bound up with the flourishing livestock industry of these regions. Not infrequently, their activities went beyond the limits of local commerce. In the tiny community of Saint-Loup lived a certain Pierre Garet, a merchant-tanner, whose wealth was so great that the citizens of Poitiers called on him whenever they needed large amounts of capital; he was even able to purchase bonds from the Hôtel de Ville of Paris. As a rule, though, the rural merchant remained an undistin- guished figure who, as might be expected, practiced usury and, in gen- eral, made money in any way possible. With a minimum of resources and the slyness of a peasant, he could go far, provided he was lucky, had very few scruples, and—as was sometimes the case—possessed a real genius for business.

SHOPKEEPERS AND HABERDASHERS

From this rural base, we move on to the urban groundwork, and here too our starting point is the market. Each town harbored a small army of shopkeepers, retailers, and hucksters, most of whom, along with the artisans, belonged to the world of the guilds, of which we know so little. The chronicles resound with the clamor of their disputes: haberdashers battled with drapers and hatters with haberdashers, whenever the latter imported and sold foreign-made articles, to the detriment of local manu- facturers. All this seems a far cry from "big business." But there were shops and there were shops. Detailed topographical studies reveal the presence of spacious storerooms next to the tiniest shops. Nor, by and large, was this sector characterized by the absence of mobility; it did allow of the concentration of capital, and it sheltered and sustained the slow, steady rise of a few individuals, like Heinrich Dunkelgud of Lü- beck, in the closing years of the fifteenth century. Having inherited from his father-in-law both the premises and stock-in-trade of two haberdash-

eries, Dunkelgud proceeded to acquire a third shop and then an establishment by the river; he salted herring there, which he imported himself
and sold both wholesale and retail. He formed a partnership with a
native of Stockholm and had a correspondent in Bruges. Another case
in point, from the annals of Freiburg: it concerns a merchant who, at
the time of his death in 1569, owned three shops, two of which were
located in neighboring towns; his total inventory was valued at 1800
florins.

Generally speaking, we know a good deal about the wide variety of
social situations that were subsumed under the term "haberdasher."
Some of the leading businessmen of Antwerp came under this heading.
In France, there was a distinction between the wholesale haberdashers
(grossiers) and the others. In Frankfurt and Erfurt, many occupied a very
honorable position on the tax rolls. But more important than the subtle-
ties and nuances of terminology is the fact that there were actually
shopkeepers whose activities went far beyond the limits of local commerce. It was customary for these people to sell anything and everything,
as witness the following posthumous inventory (drawn up in 1566) of
a Hanseatic haberdasher in Rostock: approximately 250 items, mostly
fabrics and garments ranging from hats to slippers, but also paper, arms,
grain, and spices. In most cases, the quantities are not very large—
twenty or thirty pounds of sugar, pepper, or anise, for example—although, in the case of textiles, they were not inconsiderable. The stock
also included thread, buttons, playing cards, and spectacles: in short,
"notions," which could be found in almost any haberdashery, along with
soap, lamps, fish, wax. Or even books and *objets d'art*, as with that
haberdasher in Görlitz (Silesia) whose account book has been preserved.
The mere existence of such a book excludes the possibility that the
merchant in question was a peddler.

Let us consider another representative of this species, Paul Meyer of
Lübeck, who, from 1583 on, was a member of the Haberdashers' Company. Upon his death in 1597, an inventory was taken. The stock was
varied, the merchandise in plentiful supply. But other items engage our

attention: the account books, numbered from 1 to 12 (unfortunately, they receive only a brief mention); a few shares, belonging to the deceased, in ships; and a long list of claims—all in all, eighty promissory notes signed by customers from Lübeck, Hamburg, Rostock, Reval, and several Danish and Swedish towns. This gives us some idea of the extent of his trade outside the local market. This "shopkeeper," like so many others, directed an enterprise whose operations, although essentially rather simple, nonetheless involved problems of credit and joint owner-ship that were not basically very different from those confronting big business.

CREDIT AND PARTNERSHIPS

As for credit, that list of eighty debtors speaks for itself. In retail transactions, and other types as well, it was customary to pay a small amount—as little as possible—in cash, and the remainder in paper: acknowledgements of debts, promissory notes, which circulated like a true currency and on which were recorded the paid installments. The notations were often made on the back of the document—hence the expression "endorse," from the Latin *dorsum*, back. These papers might or might not fix the date or dates for payment. But it often happened that the due-date came and went, and the creditor saw nothing coming in; in that case, he made certain "adjustments," fixed a final balance, and if need be, agreed to compromise. As for partnerships, we also find an illustration in the case of Paul Meyer: among his twelve account books, one was kept "in company" with another merchant, and certain claims belonged not to Meyer alone but to the company. It was a very simple company with a rather small capital fund, but even in trans-actions at this humble level, we find the seeds of business practices that are generally considered of recent origin. For example, a certain mer-chant from Mesnil–Raoul (near Rouen) sold to a merchant in Vernon "600 thousand vine-props (at a cost of 104 per 100)," to be delivered in three weeks' time, identical to those which the seller regularly displayed at the market. This may seem like a very ordinary transaction involving some pieces of wood and a mere 200 écus soleil, but all the same, we see here an example of selling through samples. Rural commerce, short-distance or medium-distance trade, represented a very considerable portion of the total circulation of wealth. One could hardly understand the men who made their living in this domain if one failed to recognize the relative complexity of their operations and the skills and calculations these required.

IV

The Businessmen

In June 1576, within the space of six days, Jehan Besse, the factor of Claude Daubray, bourgeois and municipal magistrate of Paris, chartered, in Rouen, seventeen Norman vessels, which were to pick up a shipment of salt in Brouage; it so happened that Daubray had purchased at auction the privilege of supplying salt to the public storehouse of Paris. Seventeen ships at one go, a fleet of 850 tons burden; in each contract, moreover, a provision for a high-risk loan to the ship's master (a total of 1670 livres tournois)—this was indeed a sizable operation. But details of this sort are not sufficient to characterize an enterprise, much less a whole social stratum, they allow us merely a brief glimpse of the total situation. Above the common run of merchants, there existed a class of big traders, who nevertheless did not form part of the international business aristocracy; this is the social sphere whose main features we shall now attempt to describe.

We can clarify this notion of a middle level in the business world by analyzing the fair in economic terms and then drawing certain analogies. A fair was a privileged market, and a participating merchant enjoyed a number of advantages. The security of his person and his property was guaranteed, and a special tribunal ensured that his grievances would be promptly redressed. But the principal advantage lay in the fact that he was granted tax exemptions. The local lord or sovereign hoped to attract foreign merchants in this way, and capture the region's trade; hence the bitter rivalry between Lyons and Geneva toward the end of the fifteenth century. But despite all the juridical distinctions, many fairs did not differ much from an ordinary market. During the first half of the century, fairs were held in thirty-two separate localities in the Paris area alone. Obviously, the letters patent granting certain privileges were not enough to transform a village into a major trading center, and the list of cities whose fairs were truly European in scope is not very long: Antwerp and Berg-op-Zoom, Lyons, Frankfurt and Leipzig, and the great fairs of Castile, notably Medina del Campo. At most of these fairs, both commodities and money were traded. Regional fairs, like those of Guibray in Normandy and Fontenay-le-Comte in Poitou, represented a far less significant concentration of trade; nevertheless, they did attract numerous merchants, some of whom came from far away. These fairs were midway between the local markets and the great international fairs.

It would be wrong to suppose that there existed a rigidly defined dual hierarchy of commercial institutions and realities, however, with the small traders being restricted to the local market, and so on. Every large fair was attended by a multitude of lesser merchants. At Lyons, in 1509, before the "Preserver" of fair privileges, a carter was suing one Léonard Arnoux, a merchant from Montferrand, "of whom he demands 6½ pounds which the aforesaid Arnoux owes him for the conveyance, by the aforesaid plaintiff, of a wagonload of woolen cloth from the place known as Foucaynes to this city of Lyons, to this fair, one year ago." Of course, we are not trying to measure the scope of the commercial activity of this man from the Auvergne on the basis of one wagonload of cloth; the point here is that a fair like Lyons's was something more than a meeting-place for big bankers. In any case, the fair was, in many respects, a holdover from the past. It was a moment in the life of a trading town when the exchange process was greatly intensified, and the date of the fair determined the calendar of business trips and payments. But fair or no fair, trading at every level went on all year long.

TYPES OF ENTERPRISES AND TYPES OF FORTUNES

The same notarial documents in which Claude Daubray is mentioned also contain the names of two wholesale wine merchants, Denis Chovard of Paris and his *parsonnier*, Michel Sablé of Blois, victuallers to the King for the cities of Calais and Ardres, partners by virtue of a contract signed at the Châtelet in July 1574. In the early part of February 1576, a cooper from Rouen, who served as their factor (he also worked for other merchants in this capacity), dispatched on their account nearly 160 barrels of wine on six vessels. We know also that in October 1577, he sent off another shipment of 170 large barrels, plus an additional 27 barrels at the end of the month; and there is a third entry for February 1578, this time for 333 large barrels and 6 *demi-queues*. And all this represented a mere fraction of a business that was supplied from at least four wine regions: the environs of Paris, Orléans, Burgundy, and Bordeaux. This particular approach to the subject (by far, the most feasible) —namely, ascertaining the quantities involved in any transactions discovered by chance in the process of examining mountains of notarial records—has yielded some significant results. When we read that an ironmaster from Hainaut once sold some 21,500 pounds of iron bars to a citizen of Rouen, it is safe to assume that the latter was not a small artisan. But such details, however precise, can provide no more than a fragment of the total picture. Did this iron merchant or the salt buyer Daubray whom we met earlier specialize in one branch of commerce? The victuallers, it so happens, dealt in herring as well as wine. We see, then, that, if we are to probe more deeply into the workings of an enterprise, more information appears necessary.

By assembling the widely scattered data on a certain individual, one can compose a fairly thick monograph. For example, take one Nicolas du Renel, a bourgeois from Paris who settled in Marseilles during the 1550s. From here, he maintained relations with Dieppe and Rouen, and he was shipping soap and oil to Le Havre in 1587. His connections with

Normandy point to an active interest in both herring and English pewter (of which he was the largest exporter on the Marseilles-Near East circuit between the years 1582 and 1591). But his activities did not stop there. As a member of the drapers' Compagnie des Ecarlates and of the companies exploiting the coral beds along the eastern coast of the Maghreb, he sold cloth and paper in Alexandria, whence he imported spices; and he also traded on the Syrian market. In fact, through his factor in Rouen, he developed commercial interests that spanned the Atlantic Ocean. In 1578, he furnished half the cargo for a vessel that was sailing to Brazil from Dieppe and was to bring back to Marseilles Brazil wood (used in dyeing), pepper, and cotton—not to mention birds! —then continue on to Le Havre, with three-fourths of its cargo again supplied by du Renel. In 1593, he imported wheat from Brittany and, despite the wheat shortage in Marseilles, exported some of it to Genoa. Our man was never bound by narrow horizons; but at the European level, he was probably not considered a businessman of the first rank. It would be interesting to compare his gross income with that revealed in R. Doucet's study of Dominique de Laran, a merchant-draper from Toulouse, for two very different kinds of commerce are involved here. Laran, whenever the opportunity presented itself, would trade in iron, wheat, horses, or even pastel, but his specialty was fabrics—woolen cloth, silk goods, and linen—which he purchased wholesale in Languedoc, Rouen, Paris, and Lyons, and then resold either retail or in small wholesale lots. There were none of the rare items of foreign trade, but nevertheless, his business extended to all the major trading towns of France—apparently without the benefit of licensed correspondents. His factors, each carrying four or five thousand livres in specie or paper money, would go out to make purchases, while others, who were sometimes partners in the firm and lived in small towns in the Southwest, would handle part of the selling. During the 1540s, his average turnover exceeded 20,000 livres tournois a year. However, for the merchant world as a whole during this period, comparable figures are lacking, for the most part. Particularly in the case of the largest firms, as we shall see, although inventories provide us with data on the amount of capital invested and the total value of their stocks, we are generally unable to make even a reasonable estimate of their annual gross income, since their account books have been lost.

Let us turn now to the situation at the other end of the continent, where the economic framework was radically different. Examining the records left by a few merchants (whose businesses were not among the largest in their community), G. Mickwitz has calculated that their annual volume was somewhere between thirty and forty thousand Riga marks (a very plausible figure)—that is, the equivalent, more or less, of the 20,000 livres tournois earned by our merchant from Toulouse in a totally unrelated branch of commerce.

Tallin was immersed in the traditional commercial activities of the Baltic region: exporting furs, hides, flax, hemp, and grain to Lübeck and the Low Countries; importing salt, woolen cloth, herring, and luxury items; and handling most of the two-way traffic between Russia and the markets of the West. Thus, a business in this area had to be organized along different lines from a draper's business in Toulouse. In particular, it was necessary to establish a solid network of contacts in foreign countries. Johann Selhorst and Tonnis Smidt, for example, both formed companies in which one or several Lübeck merchants were partners; by 1530 or 1540, their annual gross income matched the figures cited above. Between 1500 and 1510, the Popplaus, Breslau merchants who dealt mostly in cloth, were grossing anywhere from 9,000 to 22,000 Hungarian florins a year; the lower figure was not quite the equivalent of the amounts mentioned in the previous illustration.

It would be worth our while to compare these enterprises, for which the documentation is relatively abundant, with those cited earlier, which have left only a few fleeting traces. Our merchants in Tallin, average importers by that city's standards, received, at the most, 100 to 200 lasts of salt a year; whatever the exact equivalence between a last and a ton, that is far less than the amount purchased in a single transaction by the factor of the Parisian Claude Daubray. (It is true, however, that for the latter, salt was the principal commodity while for the former, it represented only a part of their trade.) The fabric trade offers another basis for comparison: in 1545, Laran bought a total of 2,785 ells of cloth, almost as much silk, and about 800 ells of linen. Chance has graciously bequeathed us a list, reproduced in a book by O. de Smedt, of the "Merchant Adventurers" who had imported cloth to Antwerp for the fair of May 1535 (hence the quantities involved represented only a fraction of their annual volume). Of the 114 names on the list, about half were down for between 100 and 500 pieces of cloth, 6 for between 500 and 1,000 pieces, 3 for between 1,000 and 2,000, and finally, 3 for more than 2,000 pieces. The last mentioned included Richard and John Gresham, father and uncle of the famous Thomas Gresham. At least half of the English merchants on this list would have to be ranked higher than a Dominique de Laran.

If the similarities and contrasts between all these figures are a fairly reliable index of the hierarchy of mercantile wealth, dare we, on this basis, reconstruct the social milieu comprising all of these merchants, who are clearly not in the same category with the top international businessmen, but whose activities, nonetheless, were not confined to one region or even, as was often the case, one country? We are not on firm ground here for too many elements are missing for us to determine the size of their fortunes, the composition of which varied considerably, or to make a comparative study of their styles of life. When he died in 1572, Jehan Pocquelin of Beauvais, putative great-grandfather of Molière, was, in the words of Pierre Goubert, a "fine merchant with an excellent stock of cloth and quality serges"—an image which brings to mind his contemporary in the Midi, Dominique de Laran. He left behind in his own house some 2,000 livres' worth of merchandise, and notes representing more than 11,000 livres in claims, and that was by no means the extent of his wealth. But let us compare these figures with those in the posthumous inventory of Paul Meyer of Lübeck. His total claims, in 1597, amounted to nearly 15,000 Lübeck marks—putting him in the same income group as Pocquelin. (At the end of the century, 8

Lübeck marks were the equivalent of approximately 7 livres tournois, or 1 livres de gros* in Flemish currency.) However, it should be pointed out that, in Lübeck, Meyer was certainly no more than a figure of the second or third rank, whereas, in Beauvais, Pocquelin was a distinguished citizen of the first rank, a municipal magistrate and collector of public funds; the latter function, along with usury, gave him an additional source of personal income apart from business, properly so-called. There was still another, very important difference: our bourgeois of Beauvais owned three magnificent farms and several hundred acres of land, and Laran's situation was about the same, but the haberdasher of Lübeck had nothing of the sort. This brings up the difficult question of the relationship between commercial activity and landed power. Depending on the extent of the latter, two equal gross incomes might well reflect very different situations.

We can thus distinguish two types among the leading "average" merchants—if this term is acceptable. One type—the highest grade of rural merchant, as it were—had a rather limited scope in his commercial activities, but devoted considerable effort to the development of his landed property. The other was more involved in long-distance expeditions, and hence more likely to settle in the maritime cities (this does not mean that he was always indifferent to the security offered by real estate investments).

FORMS OF ORGANIZATION

The importance of this distinction must not be exaggerated, but it did manifest itself in the organizations of these two types of enterprise. Dominique de Laran required the services of rather numerous factors, but whether buying or selling, his operations were not very complex. For the merchants of Marseilles who traded with the Near East or for those

---

*The livre de gros was a money of account used by merchants in Flanders, worth 6 livres, and a sous de gros was worth 6 sous, a denier de gros worth 6 deniers.

in the heart of the Baltic region who traded with the Low Countries, distance alone posed difficult problems. These could be resolved by sending out commercial travelers while the master remained at the headquarters of his firm. In the case of the Hermite brothers of Marseilles, one brother would make frequent trips to the Near East, specifically to Aleppo or Tripoli; when he returned home, a compatriot of his would be left in charge of his affairs in Syria. Some German merchants had factors stationed permanently in the Low Countries. Others employed licensed correspondents acting as commissioned agents—innkeepers frequently discharged this function on a more or less regular basis. And finally, two merchants living in widely separated areas might serve each other as commissioned agents—this was the simplest form of a type of company, which became very widespread. In fact, diversity of form was evident in the basic structures of the commercial companies. The purpose of forming a partnership was either to augment the available capital or to facilitate relations between distant points. The partners did not always relinquish their autonomy.

To entrust the handling of one's affairs in a distant place not to a mere factor, but to an unequal partner sharing in the profits, was the idea behind the old Italian *commenda*, a typically Mediterranean institution, which might have been the inspiration for a partnership established in La Rochelle in 1599 (the contract appears in a book by E. Trocmé and M. Delafosse).

The company had a capital of 1,500 écus in the form of merchandise, 1,200 put up by Jacques Guillemard of La Rochelle and 300 by Jehan Bouet of Montpellier. The latter was placed in charge of selling, "for the betterment, benefit, and profit of their aforesaid company, whether in the region of Bordeaux, Toulouse, or elsewhere, by land or by sea." After this, Bouet would have to go to Marseilles, "in order that, arriving in that place with the aforesaid funds, the aforesaid Bouet should have them conveyed to the countries of Egypt or Syria, as he sees fit, or else engage a qualified representative to make the required purchase in the aforementioned region of Alexandria."

In Marseilles, Bouet was to take out insurance on a portion of the funds; and, on returning to the city, he was to dispose of the merchandise he had purchased in the Near East. He pledged "to render a good and faithful account of the handling and the negotiation of the entire transaction." From the proceeds of this sale, upon his return each partner would first deduct his share of the capital, and then the profits would be distributed, two-thirds to Guillemard, one-third to Bouet. This proportion would also apply in the sharing of all expenses.

The inferior status of Bouet, who was the *socius tractans* in this partnership, is also shown by the fact that he could "under no circumstances, negotiate any business nor have this done through an intermediary, unless all the proceeds therefrom accrued to the benefit and profit of the aforesaid contracting parties," that is, the company. On the other hand, there was nothing to prevent Guillemard from engaging in similar or different trading activities with other partners. Finally, it is important to note the occasional character of this "company": it was based on a single expedition, and once accounts were settled, the contract became null and void on July 24, 1600.

In other cases, a merchant might advance a certain sum of money to a factor or to a young associate who was willing to put up an equal amount. However, under such an arrangement, the partnership, whether occasional or permanent in character, was, in principle, an unequal one. A company formed by several merchants from different areas, in which control was to be shared equally by all the partners— (or, at least, proportionally to the amount of capital contributed by each) —could also help to overcome the problem of distance. The guiding principle of such an association was reciprocity for services rendered. This can be seen from the following document, cited by Mickwitz (because of its brevity, we have translated almost literally):

In God's name, amen. We, the undersigned, Tonnis Smidt, Markus Smidt, Pawel Ronnefelth acknowledge that in the year 1547 in September, Tonnis Smidt came to Lübeck and treated with Pawel Ronnefelth on behalf of his brother Markus Smidt for the purpose of forming a company among us three. And in God's name we reached an agreement in October to begin a merchandising enterprise that would extend both eastwards and westwards, between Lübeck and Reval, Narva and Dorpat, by sea or by land, as we shall deem fit. To this end, each of us pledges 2000 Riga marks, to wit: Tonnis Smidt 2000 m., Markus Smidt 2000 m., Pawel Ronnefelth 2000 m., in all 6000 Riga marks. . . .

There is no mention of an expiration date, nor are the relationships between the members specifically defined. But each member knew what was expected of him, each would be working one end of the line, both for the company's account and for himself. In effect, their individual enterprises would remain separate entities.

A large number of companies brought together—often within the more or less broad framework of a family—a majority, if not all, of the merchant population of the same town; this was apparently the case with the Larans and the Popplaus. This same desire to enlarge the capital fund and share the risks also led to the establishment, independently of family connections, of *parsonneries*, which were either confined to strictly local trading or else became involved in distant adventures (here again, from another angle, the problem of distance). Were these companies merely temporary arrangements? In the quaintly worded contract (reproduced in Strieder) signed in Antwerp in 1535, Hans Papenbruch of Aix-la-Chapelle, Anselm Odeur of Bois-le-Duc, Pierre Rousse of Arras, Gérard Paul of Aix-la-Chapelle, Nicolas de Marretz of Tournai, "hereby promise and pledge, each to the other and all together, that they will very diligently, loyally, and to the best of their ability undertake and exercise the conduct and style of merchandising and make a journey to Spain." They put up 75, 65, 100, 40, and 20 livres de gros respectively, and all expenditures and profits were to be shared proportionally. In order to limit expenses, "each of the five shall dress and clothe himself respectably and not too extravagantly, in such manner as he ordinarily does and as his state and condition require."

No one was to engage in trading on the outside. Papenbruch and Odeur were named the "chiefs and principals"; they would be in charge of the treasury, in which one-eighth of the capital would be kept, while the remainder was to be invested in merchandise. They were to report on the company's finances every two weeks. There was still another clause warning against prodigality: it was agreed that "food will be purchased at the lowest possible prices," that whoever wanted better fare "will be required to pay for such out of his own purse, as shall also be the case for banquets or anything else which exceeds the ordinary."

And furthermore: "if, moreover, it so happened that, after their departure from this place, Antwerp, on the way to Spain, and thus during the term of this company, any one of them were to find himself in some dissolute place and were to be wounded or grievously harmed or were to indulge in certain excesses, such as gambling or associating with wanton women, or other such eventualities, he will be required to suffer the cost and the penalties and to pay himself any fines imposed." If, while in Spain, they learned, "by making inquiries of the men of property of the country, that it would not be profitable to go to the province of Peru," they were to sell and liquidate their merchandise in Spain. But if instead it seemed advisable to "move on and make their voyage to the province of Peru, where they would make a better profit," they would set sail, with the intention of remaining there for at least one year or, in any case, until they had sold all their merchandise.

And, finally, we come to what is no doubt the root of the matter: "Likewise: if it so happened that, while they were in Peru or elsewhere, they or any one of them were to be in some place where he found some pieces of, or matter containing, gold, silver, precious stones, or jewels, they or he will be bound to bring them back and distribute them equally among all the aforesaid partners, without regard to the amount that they invested in the aforesaid company." If Peru was in the midst of "some war against the infidels and if there were one among the aforesaid company who wished to take part in a foray against the aforesaid infidels . . . and if, by chance, the aforesaid partner were to win some wealth from the aforesaid infidels, he will keep for himself no more than the third part of that which he has won," the remaining two-thirds going to his associates, even if they had refused to risk their lives by joining him in this venture.

As we see, there are provisions covering everything, even the extra-commercial aspects of the venture; for even a simple operation could easily become submerged in a morass of complications. Admittedly, the circumstances surrounding this affair were unusual. In 1535, Antwerp was atremble with the latest news from Peru, and more than one bold fellow among the lowliest merchants was dreaming of the most fabulous coups.

Another type of company, with a more elaborate structure, is revealed in another contract, drawn up in Antwerp in 1550. The two contracting parties, one from Antwerp and the other from London, agreed to com-mit all their wealth for a period of seven years; during this time neither would be allowed to engage in trading independently of the company. Every two years, accounts would be settled, and after six years, they would decide whether or not they wished to extend the contract for another seven years. Each was entitled to 35 Flemish livres per year for living expenses; all other expenses would be borne jointly. In this specific case of a solidly unified structure, we can recognize the influence of the far more complex patterns evolved by the largest mercantile companies. Let us go to Antwerp: The great Coral Company of the Seas of Bône, which was founded in Marseilles in 1553 and lasted until the end of the century, with several partners each owning a more or less significant portion of the 25 carats, or shares, represented, in certain respects, a more sophisticated setup. But it did not have a fixed capital fund; money had to be raised for every operation. And when the processed coral had been exchanged for spices in Alexandria, each member could do as he wished with his share of the proceeds. The partnership was thus an imperfect one.

On the whole, at this middle level of the business world, which we have attempted to reconstruct, the structures of the non-individual enterprises were marked by a certain fluidity, and in many respects bore a striking resemblance to the business practices of the small merchants.

It should be enough to recall the selling procedures and methods of payment in order to illustrate the continuity in technique—which was an expression of the economic, social, and psychological continuity— between the lower and the higher levels of commerce. Whenever a transaction was concluded, there was the same assortment of stipulations, sometimes very complicated; and the same strong aversion to paying cash. But to the extent that the quantities in question were much larger and could no longer be delivered in a single shipment, it was necessary to resort to written contracts, which were either notarized or handled by a broker. Exports of cloth from London to Antwerp, shipments of rye to Portugal, and deliveries of salt were often negotiated in this manner.

Credit inevitably played an essential role in these operations. By signing a promissory note for part or all of the amount in question, the purchaser avoided parting with any of his cash for an indefinite period. He could settle his debts by using his own credits—cash serving mainly for the liquidation of final balances. Along with this rather provincial procedure, the "average" merchants also utilized the letter of exchange, a device perfected two centuries earlier by the merchant-bankers of Italy. And this brings us to the threshold of the world of big business.

V

The Business Aristocracy

The basis of all banking activity in the sixteenth century, as in earlier periods, was the practice of money-changing. Banking offered the possibility of making profits over and above those made in merchandising, and it is from this angle that we should try to visualize it. For simplicity's sake, we shall leave aside the deposit banks, which, as a form of private enterprise, retained their importance only in Spain. Let us begin, then, with an analysis of an exchange operation. The text of the following letter, sent to Rouen from Antwerp in 1576, is a classic example of a letter exchange:

Laus Deo. For the sum of 853 livres, 4 sous tournois. Pay by this first [letter] of exchange, [we] having paid by the second [letter] a week after presentation to Sr. François Delobel the sum of eight hundred fifty-three livres and four sous tournois in good currency that is in circulation among merchants, in exchange for 100 livres de gros here received from Sr. Steven Ractret. Make good payment and charge to our account as stated in letter of notification. Issued in Antwerp this 18th day of April in the year fifteen hundred seventy-six.

Jehan de Voss and company.

On the back: "To Sr. Jehan Deudemar, merchant residing on the rue Escuyère in Rouen."

As can be seen from this text, an exchange transaction customarily involved four persons: the "giver" or "bailor" (the resident of Antwerp who furnished the 100 livres de gros); the "drawer" or "taker" (the man who received these 100 livres de gros in exchange for the letter he had signed, Jehan de Voss); the "drawee," the drawer's correspondent (the Rouen merchant who had to pay the amount stated in the letter in French currency—P. Deudemar); and, finally, the "beneficiary," the bailor's correspondent (in this case, Delobel). One obvious feature of this transaction is that it involved a transfer of funds from one place to another (*distantia loci*, in the language of theologians) and from one currency to another (*permutatio pecuniae*). Originally, these two conditions were in principle indispensable if the operation was to be deemed licit under canon law. But by the sixteenth century, it was common practice to draw letters of exchange, not only within a particular monetary zone, but even within the confines of a single town. Another feature, which is not readily observable, has come to light through the research of Raymond de Roover: the exchange contract involves a credit operation in conjunction with the transfer. By putting up a certain amount of specie, the bailor became a creditor in the foreign trading town, and he could utilize his credit there in various ways: he could settle a debt, apply this money to the purchase of merchandise (which would then represent his return), or else get his money back (generally, by having his correspondent send him a remittance). In any case, the circuit was complete only if an outlay of funds was followed up by a return. For the merchant-banker, who, in the beginning, usually acted as the bailor, the essence of the art of exchange was to get the largest possible return on every outlay.

The differences in exchange rates—the primary consideration in any exchange transaction—were conditioned by two factors which must be clearly distinguished. On the one hand, the exchange rate varied over time; on the other hand—and this is a very important point—there was, at any given moment, generally speaking, a disparity between, let us say, the exchange rate for Antwerp currency in Lyons and the rate for French currency in Antwerp. In both places, the rate was always expressed as so many deniers de gros per écu de marc (about eight ounces of gold or silver): at Lyons, the quoted price was the "certain"* one; at Antwerp, the "uncertain" one. The rate in the market that quoted the "certain" was higher than that in the other, and this difference was the source of the interest on the money put up by the bailor. Theoretically the bailor's profit from the transaction was always in doubt; during the interval between outlay and return, the money market might take a bad turn, so that the anticipated gain would turn into a loss. The métier had its risks, but in practice the exchange brokers could minimize them, since they were always well informed about the monetary situation in various market cities. Unforeseen disasters did occur, however (though, certainly, not everyone suffered therefrom)— one example being the famous edict issued by Henry III on November 18, 1577. To put an end to the prevailing monetary chaos, the King ordered a "reduction" of the specie, that is, a devaluation of the money of account. This was a cruel blow, since the going exchange rate for the écu was reduced from 100 sous tournois (sometimes more) to 66 sous at first, and then to 60 after January 1, 1578.

Take the case of Charles de Saldaigne, a Rouen merchant of Spanish origin. On November 16, a draft payable on sight for 1,000 écus, at 50 sous to the écu (2,500 livres tournois) was drawn on his account in London. The draft was presented to him on December 12; since the pound had been devalued, he was obliged to lay out considerably more than his correspondent, the drawer (an Italian living in London), had figured on. And so, Saldaigne "demands that the judges hear his case so that he may show how great the damages and interest would be, were he now to pay the sum of said payment, which would amount to more than forty percent interest for less than one month, which is clearly exorbitant." But this same contingency also had the effect of increasing inordinately the profit of the bailor or the beneficiary. The latter, Fernando de Zarata, the factor in Rouen for the Malvendas (a very large international firm) naturally demanded payment at the rate fixed by the

---

*"Certain" = the value in French money of a foreign currency; "uncertain" = the value of foreign money expressed in terms of the money of that nation, i.e., Antwerp.

decree (which was to his advantage). He pointed out that this sum constituted the return on his investment; he "had forwarded said money" from Rouen to London, when the going rate was 47 deniers sterling for an écu of 50 sous, and "got the return of his said money in this city of Rouen at 42." Thus, the whole transaction, "which had taken more than four months, during which time he had run the risk of falling into debt," had netted him a profit of about 10 percent. The discrepancy between the two methods of calculating is easily explained: the beneficiary sought to minimize the effects of the monetary revaluation. But that the money put up by the bailor should earn interest was considered perfectly normal.

For a good many merchants, exchange was, above all, either a means of obtaining credit (through the use of drafts) in a particular trading-town or a sure way of obtaining funds for making commercial payments abroad. For the merchant-bankers, who were mainly Italians, it represented a purely speculative activity. By purchasing letters of exchange, these people were able to make their capital bear fruit in the money market—without always obeying the complex but flexible restrictions that theologians sought to impose on certain operations. For there were all sorts of fictitious exchanges, "dry" exchanges, and so on, devised to eliminate all risk, absolutely guaranteeing a profit determined in advance —which made the lender's purse, if not his conscience, more secure. Let us consider only one variety: the "deposit" or fair-to-fair exchange, which was employed at Lyons, Antwerp, and the Genoese fairs. In practice, it amounted to an interest loan payable at the time of the subsequent fair in the same town, and could thus be renewed every three months. The financial practices of the sixteenth century did not include discounting letters of exchange; the latter could not even be transferred without going through certain formalities. The first known examples of the endorsed letter of exchange date from the fifteenth century, but endorsement was an innovation that was not used very frequently until the end of the sixteenth century. The instrument itself had not yet acquired the flexibility it would eventually possess; nevertheless, what-

ever its form—legitimate or otherwise—it offered a marvelous means for
"making money work." Obviously, the merchants who made use of it
had to possess technical knowledge far more subtle than that required
for "the conduct and style" of ordinary merchandising. Upon receiving
a draft, the beneficiary presented it to the drawee, who, having been
notified in writing by the drawer, was obliged to "accept" the draft and
make payment within the specified time limit. At the fairs, where an
exceedingly large number of letters were handled, the bankers, once they
had obtained the requisite acceptances, proceeded to "clear the notes"
—a process which a contemporary explained in his own peculiar fashion
as follows: "On the one hand, you owe me money and, on the other,
I owe you money; let us consolidate; and so-and-so owes you money and
I owe him money, and you owe me money; let us consolidate and pay
each other."

The result: very large sums of money were transferred while very little
cash changed hands. From 1570 to 1580 the Bonvisi of Lucca, operating
as bankers in Lyons, paid out at every fair, for their clients and for their
own account, sums on the order of 300,000 écus.

MONOPOLIES AND CARTELS

However, even when trafficking in money became their principal
activity, the big businessmen kept up their merchandising operations.
But these operations were conducted on a scale and under conditions
such that an organization and methods analogous to those employed in
banking were required. In the first place, a network of correspondents,
covering not only a few foreign trading towns but a very large number
of commercial centers, was indispensable. Whether the aim was to
speculate on the money market or to procure great quantities of spices,
alum, textiles, or metal products, it was essential—if the conduct of the
enterprise was to be rationalized—to keep abreast of the trends in all
the leading markets.

From this point of view, a sharp difference arose between those whose operations were confined to a certain geographical area and the very large firms whose predominance was universal. In 1525, at Antwerp, Joachim Pruner, a German merchant from Berlin, founded a company with Kilian Rietwieser. The latter, who had left Wurzburg to settle in Leipzig, belonged, it would appear, to that average class of businessmen that we examined earlier, and his territory lay between central Germany and Antwerp. Pruner operated on a larger scale: an importer of spices and gems from Portugal, he was also involved in Antwerp's financial activities. Each partner brought the other new outlets and new sources of supplies, and when combined, their respective enterprises complemented each other, forming a continuous chain stretching from Lisbon to Leipzig, with headquarters in Antwerp. At a higher level, even the Fuggers resorted to forming partnerships in order to penetrate a market, but once their stake in a particular region had become fairly large, they established direct representation; and their network covered every important trading town. During the 1520s, the Welsers (Augsburg branch) had permanent representatives in Nuremberg, Milan, Venice, Rome, Bern, Zurich, Freiburg, Lyons, Antwerp, Lisbon, and Saragossa. Or consider the Bonvisi—without a doubt, the biggest bankers in Lucca—with flourishing operations going in England and the Low Countries; their headquarters were in Lyons, and they had numerous branch offices and correspondents throughout France, Italy, and Spain. Dozens of other firms disposed similar networks, the contours of which were subject to continual modification.

The uniqueness of the largest enterprises lay in the scope of their operations. A few statistics on the Fuggers' activities in the copper industry will give the reader some idea of what was considered enormous during this period. Between 1500 and 1540, they shipped at least 10,000 quintals (hundredweights) of copper a year, sometimes much more, from Danzig to Antwerp. There were times when they had as much as 20,000 quintals, or even more, in their Antwerp warehouses. In their 1527 inventory, this copper stock in Antwerp, with an estimated value of more than 200,000 florins, represented more than half their total stock of merchandise; their total assets amounted to approximately 3 million florins. By 1546, their assets stood at 7.1 million and their total stock was valued at 1.25 million, including one million florins in copper and 125,000 in fustian. It is not hard to imagine that the volume of sales must have been correspondingly great. In 1548, for example, a three-year contract was concluded with their Portuguese factor in Antwerp for 7,500 quintals of brass bracelets, to be sent to Africa, and more than 40,000 cauldrons and other utensils made from the same metal, also to be delivered to Lisbon for eventual use in the "Guinea trade."

Such gigantic stocks and enormous transactions were more often than not made possible by the possession of a monopoly—exclusive privileges granted by a sovereign. Intervention by the state was not the sole determining factor, of course: a firm's chances of obtaining a monopoly depended on the scope of its commercial power and hence on its ability to render the prince in question certain services. But in the economy of the sixteenth century, it was not possible to establish a veritable monopoly except in certain relatively restricted sectors which, for various reasons, were under royal jurisdiction.

The classic example was the spice trade. When the first fleets bound for the Indies were fitted out, the contributions made by the largest foreign firms in Lisbon were essential. The Italians, in particular, attracted to Portugal by African gold and already involved in the sugar trade with the islands, knew how to profit from this opportunity. When the fleet returned, they received their share of the spices; having invested 2,000 ducats in Vasco da Gama's second voyage, Gian Francesco Affaitadi came away with 5,000 ducats' worth of spices. Subsequently, when the royal monopoly was organized, two separate contracts were drawn up: one for the procurement of the spices in the Indies and delivery to the Casa, the other for their sale throughout Europe. The difference between the import price and the export price constituted the King's profit. For the contracting parties, the principal advantage of the operation was that it assured them of a virtual monopoly. From 1508 to 1514, the Gualterotti and the Affaitadi were the only ones authorized to sell the royal spices in the Low Countries. Later on, Germans and, above all, Portuguese Marranos, played a decisive role in exploiting this monopoly, which provoked protests from the consumers. Occasionally, there was some friction between the contracting parties, for once Venetian spices were back on the market, Portugal's spices no longer enjoyed their privileged position. In spite of these vicissitudes, the contracts in question continued to attract large firms. Around 1580, a German named Konrad Rott came to grief when he tried to corner both the Asian and European contracts; and the contracts of 1586 and 1591, which involved the Milanese Rovelasca, the Welsers, and the Fuggers, were also, as we know from detailed accounts, great disappointments, mainly owing to the hazards of sea travel. (Several individuals had participated in hopes of recovering certain claims from the Spanish monarchy, which had been jeopardized by the latter's bankruptcy in 1575.) At this late date, the spice market ceased to offer the big entrepreneurs the exceptional opportunities for profit-making which had existed fifty years before.

The mechanism behind the equally enormous transactions in the metals industry was of a different order, although the basic circumstances were similar: impecunious sovereigns working hand-in-glove with merchants on the lookout for big profits. Exploited by artisan miners, who sometimes banded together in primitive guilds, the mines produced considerable revenue in kind for the prince or lord to whom they belonged (by virtue of the fact that the subsoil was royal property). In order to mobilize this wealth, they called on the merchants. The frequency and the scale of the operations in this industry during the sixteenth century were unprecedented. Merchants made loans to the sovereign that could be repaid in metal or were guaranteed by liens on the income from the mines. After all, were not the merchants in the best position to handle these products on the international market? Consider the Fuggers, the Welsers, and the Paumgartners, all of whom sold the metals produced in central Europe in Venice and Antwerp. Between 1496 and 1544, Hans Paumgartner of Augsburg and his son Hans made numerous "silver purchases" from the Habsburgs; for a total of almost 600,000 florins lent, they received about 440,000 marks (in weight) of the white metal. The Fuggers did even better with copper from the Tyrol, Carinthia, and Hungary; from 1495 to 1548, they possessed a veritable mining monopoly in all three regions.

The exploitation of the Pope's alum deposits was conducted under similar arrangements. Moreover, to ward off competition from Turkish alum, the Holy See had recourse to spiritual weapons—which proved rather ineffective, however. The concessionaires took more comfort from the Apostolic Chamber's resolution, made in 1531, to prohibit the exploitation of all mines except those in La Tolfa—the ones named in their contract.

The struggle against competition also led to the establishment of cartels. The purpose of the copper syndicate created in 1498 through an agreement between the firms of Fugger, Gossembrot, Herwart, and Paumgartner was to keep the price of the metal on the Venetian market at a certain level, determined by precise calculation. The Fuggers' factor in Venice was charged with selling for all four parties. (Another copper syndicate was set up in 1534, this time in Thuringia, by businessmen with interests in the Mansfeld mines.) The whole operation involved maneuvers which suggest a cutthroat battle between rival interest groups, and have a very modern flavor. In fact, at that time (1498), Fugger's competitors in Augsburg were disturbed about the sudden upswing in Hungary's output; with the help of Maximilian, who thought he could gain from this affair, they compelled Fugger to sign the agreement, hoping to trap him by neutralizing his Hungarian copper holdings. Fugger acknowledged the blow without batting an eyelash, for he had prepared a counterstroke. His "Hungarian commerce" was handled by a company uniting the Fuggers and the Thurzos; actually, Fugger was in control, and officially, the Hungarian copper was not part of their "joint commerce." So he competed with the syndicate, of which he was a member, by selling the Hungarian copper at a lower price. The stratagem of the syndicate's promoters had boomeranged, and the Fuggers' position was consolidated.

Another agreement, concluded in 1548, between Anton Fugger and Mathäus Manlich, who had just taken over the lease on the Hungarian mines, was prompted by different motives. It was a matter of sharing markets, for the Fuggers still had enormous copper stocks as well as other mines. Hence the text stipulated, in very precise language, the rights that each accorded the other in Spain, Portugal, France, and so on; it also stated that the price current in the Low Countries was to be maintained, and that if either of the parties lowered this price, he would have to pay the other a penalty sum.

It would seem, then, that the fear of competition and the preoccupation with protection that characterize the guild mentality also guided the actions of the big entrepreneurs, who knew how to pass off their maneuvers as defensive measures, which they sought to justify in terms of the city's or country's general interests. Thus, in 1527, the counts of Mansfeld, in league with some Nuremberg businessmen, tried to exclude the Saxons from their copper trade—a move which provoked the ire of Leipzig merchants who were not party to the Mansfeld combine. These merchants then drew the city's attention to all the dangers which threatened it—deserted fairs, for instance, and competition from Prague. "To avert these, according to God's will, it is deemed good and necessary that we apply ourselves energetically to securing for the inhabitants of Leipzig the rights to the lead of Goslar, the copper and silver of Bohemia, the zinc of Schlackenwald and the zinc in the principality of Saxony, all of which should be placed in the same hands." This proposed counterattack was, in effect, a neat monopolization scheme; if it had been carried out, it probably would have benefited a mere handful of individuals.

When big business moved into areas that directly affected the common people—the salt or grain market, for example—its practices usually aroused the consumers' hostility. The Grand Parti du sel, formed in France in 1585, is an outstanding example of those combines that arose during periods of scarcity. A small group, which included Charles de

Saldaigne and the very big Italian financier Zamet, assumed in a leased contract the task of supplying the entire kingdom with salt, which was to be imported from the Iberian Peninsula. Things did not turn out as well as could be expected. One reason, no doubt, was that it was necessary to charter a fleet of 30,000 tons.

In every branch of commerce, as in banking, the big businessman employed the same distinctive modus operandi. But the traffic in ordinary foodstuffs was remarkably unpredictable. There was always the danger, for example, of a bad harvest; it was more difficult to predict— or to arrange for—periods of scarcity and periods of abundance in the grain market than in the money market. The products subject to monopolization were in an intermediate category; hence, the sixteenth century had its "kings" of copper, of spices, or of banking, who showed little interest in humbler commodities, which they gladly left to lesser lords.

THE MERCHANT AND PUBLIC FINANCE

The granting of monopolies was only one aspect of the close relationship between the political authorities and the business world. The onerous tasks merchants performed for their sovereigns can be divided into two categories: tax-farming and loans. Certain operations, moreover, combined both services; thus, by way of paying back a loan, a sovereign might grant a merchant a collectorship for a period of a few years. The tax-farming system drew merchants from every stratum of the business community, for the lowliest lay or ecclesiastical lord, urban communities, and kings, all preferred employing intermediaries for the purpose of collecting their various revenues. There was never a shortage of candidates, whether the assignment was the "inspection and sealing of cloth," the "tax on fresh, dry, and salted herrings" at the municipal level, or the *"maestrazgos,"* which were the royal revenues from Spain's three great orders of knighthood. Whether a small merchant or a powerful financier, everyone could find a tax farm that suited his tastes or his means. Thus, in 1576, a merchant–butcher was in charge of collecting "the excise tax on the cloven hoof: 10 sous for each steer, 5 sous for each cow, 2 sous 6 deniers for each hog, and 18 deniers for each calf, ewe, or ram brought in to the city and suburbs of Rouen." This was a rather profitable farm, taking in 9,650 livres tournois a year; whereas in that same year and same district, the levy on wholesale wine (6 deniers per queue) brought in only 130 livres. Moreover, the collector always had the right to take on partners or to divide up his tax farm among several subcontractors. Thus, in every province, bailliage, and small district, there was a pyramid of lease holders.

From the rural merchant who took a collectorship worth a few écus to the Italian banker (such as the Luccan, Lodovico Diaceto) who secured the customs dues of Lyons for himself—amounting to 190,000 livres a year—the basic principle was the same; only the volume of the receipts varied with the influence of the contractor. At Nantes, a certain Julien Ruiz, one of the city's leading merchants, collected tax farms of every sort: municipal farms worth a few thousand livres, those of the provostship (customs dues), as well as the one for royal tolls in Brittany (which totaled 170,000 livres a year in 1576). At this high level, the assumption of a collectorship always involved a large advance: such arrangements were major financial dealings.

However, furnishing credit in the form of loans was one step above all this and fell within the exclusive domain of the real money magnates. The needs of the sovereigns were always far in excess of their resources, however abundant those might be, and systems of public credit—like the bonds of the Hôtel de Ville in France or the *juros* in Spain—were just coming into existence. These particular forms of long-term borrowing, inspired by the examples long set by the municipal authorities, put the latter in the unenviable role of intermediaries; for as far as the aspiring rentiers were concerned, the cities' credit was better than the king's. But in order to make up the tremendous deficits that continually undermined the royal treasuries, still more expedients were required; for one, it was necessary to obtain short-term loans from the bankers.

In the very first years of the century, this sort of transaction was very artisanal in nature, involving no more than a few thousand écus, ducats, or florins; even the loans made to the Habsburgs by large firms like the Paumgartners' remained at this level for quite some time. But with the help of the large fairs such as those at Lyons and Antwerp, people were soon counting—or juggling, it seemed—by the hundreds of thousands. The imperial crown of 1519 can almost be considered a modest purchase when compared with the astronomical sums represented by the bankers' claims on the sovereigns of France, England, Spain, and Portugal toward the middle of the century. Henry II owed some bankers in Lyons a good 12 million livres tournois. In the case of the Spanish Empire, which was so extensive and spread out, the problem of obtaining credit was coupled with the problem of transferring funds. American silver arrived in Seville once a year—but the date varied, owing to the uncertainties of navigation, and the payments falling due everywhere could not wait. Hence arose a practice called the *asiento:* certain businessmen took it upon themselves to obtain, for a limited period, in various trading towns (especially Antwerp), means of payment that were backed up by payments made or to be made in Spain.

There were very few firms (a few German and Italian banks) capable of taking on alone a contract for one or two million écus, as the Fuggers and Spinolas did. But the merchants who put up less impressive sums, out of caution or because their means were more limited, nevertheless emerged as important international businessmen by virtue of such operations. Generally—and this was the outstanding feature of such transactions—interest rates were very high, putting the lenders in a very advantageous position. In Lyons, toward the end of the reign of Francis I, the rate was 4 percent every three months, while in Antwerp, credit was costing Charles V 12 percent per annum. (If a government was in very desperate straits, the real interest rate, however, sometimes exceeded 20 percent.) With the *asientos,* profits varied considerably because of fluctuations in exchange rates. But as a rule, the interest on monies lent to princes was definitely higher than the going rate among merchants in the money market.

HOW GREAT WERE THE RISKS?

This higher rate would certainly have been translated into enormous profits had it not been for the far greater risks faced by creditors in dealing with debtors, who were rarely punctual when it came time to pay. For a time, these delays were an additional source of profit for the lenders. But eventually the inevitable catastrophe occurred: the French monarchy went completely bankrupt in 1559, while the Spanish government did likewise in 1557, 1575, and 1596. And all the creditors were ruined? Matters were not that simple. Naturally, each crisis left more or less seriously wounded victims. (By the way, such episodes were not the exclusive property of western Europe. In 1572, the Loitzes—the largest company in all of northern Europe—went bankrupt, mainly because they found it impossible to collect the money owed them by the sovereigns of Poland, Denmark, and Prussia.) Despite these bankruptcies, the financial operations of the big lenders did not always show an unfavorable balance.

When a sovereign failed to honor his commitments, the bankers would grant an extension only in return for irrevocable liens on the revenues of the crown. In 1555, the French monarchy, in the supreme effort to arrest the growth of its floating debt, set up the famous Grand Parti,* which, in the end, served only to postpone the fatal due date. But a bankruptcy usually produced compromise arrangements. For example, the loans might be converted to government bonds; although the interest on these was much lower, it was still a means of consolidating. If they granted further loans to the bankrupt sovereign, the more prudent businessmen brought up his old, somewhat worthless obligations, the total value of which was added, in the new debts, to the sums of money actually lent. Not everyone, however, succeeded in making good

---

*The Grand Parti was a financial syndicate created at Lyons by Tournon in 1555, by a fusion of the interests of Italian bankers. Loans to the King of France resulted in its bankruptcy after the Treaty of Cateau-Cambresis in 1559.

his losses; in 1586, for example, some Swiss offered to pay a mere 25 percent of the face value for German claims against the King of France. But no doubt a good many Italians had got out of the venture without any losses. Likewise, whenever the Spanish monarchy went bankrupt, more and more American silver poured into Genoese coffers.

In order to keep up this enormous flow of money on which the states were utterly dependent, the businessmen required quantities of capital far in excess of their own liquid assets, inasmuch as wholesale trade or manufacturing tied up considerable sums of money. This observation calls for a more thorough analysis of the origins and functions of capital.

VI

Capitalism or Capitalists?

The sixteenth century inherited its higher forms of organization from medieval Italy and did not introduce any fundamental modifications. The company remained an association of individuals. The founding group retained exclusive control of the enterprise; each member, having contributed a portion of the registered capital (called the *corpo* in Italy) and responsible for a share of the work, found himself committed, in both respects, for the duration of the contract. These full partners, few in number, were favored in the distribution of profits, which they alone determined. Thus, the company had a fixed capital and, in business relations, functioned as a single unit, clearly distinguishable from its individual members. But if the limitation of responsibility was to be the eventual outcome of these developments, the concept itself had not yet been expressly formulated. There were still strict regulations regarding the transfer of shares, in order to prevent persons not belonging to the original group from entering the company.

THE COMPANIES

One extremely important institution in the life of many companies was the shareholders' meeting which took place at the expiration of the contract. The purpose was to draw up a balance sheet, decide whether or not to renew the contract (and eventually modify the conditions and the capital fund), and make decisions concerning the organization and the management of the enterprise. Thus, in 1499, while in Lyons, the young Lucas Rem, having just completed his apprenticeship, was informed that Anton Welser, Conrad Vöhlin, and Company had hired him for a three-year period at its general session held in Augsburg. Lucas Rem's diary—which, in its references both to the author's private life and to his business activity, is one of the most illuminating documents left by a sixteenth-century merchant—gives an account of the operations of the company that he himself founded after breaking away from the Welsers in 1517. Here, for example, is how he describes the settling of accounts in 1525: "On 15 June 1525, at Augsburg, we drew up a general balance-sheet. By the grace of God, the profit came to 30%. I had 10,500 florins in capital. . . ." His profit came to 3,150 florins, to which were added allowances for expenses and other sums due him as a creditor of the company. With each reorganization, his role in the company changed, as can be seen from the entries in his diary.

In the event that the partners' funds were not sufficient to finance the enterprise, there were two ways of procuring the needed extra capital. The simpler of the two methods was to solicit deposits which offered subscribers a fixed interest rate, usually 5 percent. The depositors were nothing more than creditors, without any say in the management of the company. It is easy to see why a company, or even a private merchant, as sometimes happened, could be induced to accept deposits: as long as the rate of profit was appreciably higher than the interest rate, the arrangement was profitable. The Höchstetters were famous for their extensive use of this device. They are said to have received one million florins in deposits from subscribers belonging to every social class—not only from the nobility and the bourgeoisie, but even from peasants and servants. The chronicler to whom we owe this piece of information may have been exaggerating, for such a situation was very rare indeed.

The other method, more complicated but more frequently employed, was to invest capital in the company on a "profit and loss" basis for longer periods than the deposits. The investors were entitled to share in the profits, though at a lower rate than that enjoyed by the original partners; this is capital *fuori del corpo*. The participants could be compared to today's stockholders, the depositors to today's debenture holders, and the third category (in this case, the analogy is somewhat less valid) to today's holders of "fluctuating" debentures.

WORKING WITH OTHER PEOPLE'S MONEY

The art of presenting a balance sheet is by no means a recent development, and the distribution of profits often gave rise, during the sixteenth century, to acrimonious controversies. The general assembly of the Welser firm, in 1517, lasted far into the night; Lucas Rem is our source for this information (he himself had been told this upon returning to Augsburg from Antwerp, one week after the meeting). He feels that he has been wronged, explains at length why this is so, and concludes by characterizing the maneuvers of the directors as "looting—as far as we, the partners, are concerned; larceny—as far as the others are concerned." His testimony, no doubt, is biased. But one could easily write a whole chapter on the art of cheating one's partners.

In the exploitation of Hungarian copper, the Fuggers had been, partners with Hans Thurzo of Cracow since 1494, a remarkable entrepreneur who was in an excellent position to obtain special dispensations from the Kings of Poland and Hungary. The contract of 1496 provided for complete equality between the two parties; the profits, "down to the last florin," were to be divided equally. But, as a result of clever juggling of the markets, the situation quickly changed in the Fuggers' favor. They purchased, for their own account, the copper outputs of Danzig and Nuremberg, the prices having been prearranged to their advantage; all the profits from the subsequent sales belonged to them. All in all, they managed to earn twice as much as Thurzo.

"Making money work" is the eternal preoccupation of the businessman, but the supreme accomplishment is making other people's money work for one's own benefit. The big merchants of the sixteenth century knew how to go about it and, for this purpose, had no need of joint stock companies. It should be born in mind that the "bourses" in those days were money markets, not stock markets. "Stocks" would not come into existence until the following century—in countries which did not have especially progressive economic institutions during the sixteenth: Holland, where a rather primitive type of company predominated—based on the Hanseatic model, and England, with its "regulated companies" (the "Merchant Adventurers," for example). The latter were endowed with a legal personality, and their life span was not dependent on the fates of their individual members, but they did not represent genuine enterprises. They were rather cartels, combining certain features of the guild and the confraternity. Such organization of the companies of the sixteenth century assured their founders of adequate resources without jeopardizing their exclusive control over the enterprise.

THE STRUCTURE OF THE ENTERPRISE

When a company is based on a capital fund, its existence is not endangered by the withdrawal of one of two individuals. This was not the actual situation in the sixteenth century, but for all practical purposes, if the enterprise stood at the top of the business world, its permanence was assured, despite the limited duration of the contracts among its participants. If a member died before the contract expired, his heirs or their representatives received his share of the profits until the time of the next renewal.

In 1549, the Bonvisi bank in Lyons was registered under the following name: "Antonio and Ludovico Bonvisi"; in 1551, this became "Antonio and the heirs of Ludovico Bonvisi"; in 1564, "The heirs of Antonio and Ludovico Bonvisi," then "The heirs of Ludovico, Benito Bonvisi, and Co." Men passed away but the firm lived on.

The second problem confronting a large-scale enterprise was, so to speak, spatial in character: how to preserve unity when it had branches scattered all over Europe? There were two distinct methods for handling this problem: on the one hand, a centralized organization with foreign trading offices, on the other, a system of subsidiary companies (which proved more flexible).

The factor or foreign representative of a large company was an employee; although in a few cases (with the Welsers, for example) he owned a share in the business, more often than not, he merely drew a salary. For example, the Schetzes of Antwerp were big financiers who dealt in metals on a very large scale, possessed industrial interests in Germany, maintained business relations with Leipzig, Danzig, and Sweden, and trafficked in spices and alum—in all, engaged in a wide variety of business activities. They also owned a plantation and a sugar mill on an island off the coast of Brazil. In 1568, the man they hired to represent them there for six years was to be lodged and maintained at their expense; he was to receive an annual salary of 200 florins, payable at the end of the six year period, when accounts would be settled. There were also times when a partner in the company was put at the head of a large foreign trading office, which, in turn, controlled smaller agencies. In any case, the system was rather clumsy and had serious disadvantages. The factor was a proxy of the firm and disposed of its seal. His decisions were reviewed only after the fact. If he was too conservative or too timid, he might pass up some excellent opportunities; if he was too bold, things might be even worse; and there was always a chance that he might be unscrupulous.

Jakob the Rich of the Fugger family had his factors under control, but under Anton, their Antwerp office got completely out of hand. The factor in charge, Veit Hörl, was personally responsible for this; he got the firm involved in enormous deals with the King of England. From 1555 to 1557, Mathäus Oertel, his successor, risked even more by granting gigantic loans to Philip II. The firm found itself on the verge of the abyss when this monarch went bankrupt—contrary to the predictions of Oertel, whose boundless optimism was, no doubt, not disinterested. In 1566, Thomas Gresham was congratulating himself on having obtained a very large loan from the Welsers' factor in Antwerp: here is further proof of the factors' independence despite the centralization policy of the chiefs at headquarters.

In order to augment their capital, the Welsers were not afraid to take on partners outside their family. The Fuggers, on the contrary, preferred to rely on credit in order to keep strangers out of the business; that is why, in Antwerp around 1540, they began to take in a great deal of money in deposits (called going "from fair to fair" in the sixteenth-century money market). Their promissory notes, the *Fuggerbriefe*, were as good as gold, but eventually they would constitute an overwhelming mass of liabilities. The problem was the same in both families: the trading offices were not bringing in very much fresh capital.

The subsidiary system offers a striking contrast. A summary of C. Bauer's analysis of the structure of the Affaitadi companies exemplifies its essential features. The parent establishment in Antwerp, "Giovanni Battista Affaitadi and Co.," had capital assets of 130,000 ducats, divided up into 130 shares, 30 of which belonged to their subsidiary in Lisbon. The latter, "Giovanni Battista Affaitadi and Nicolo Giraldi and Co.," had capital assets of 97,000 ducats composed of 97 shares; 12 of these shares belonged to the "heirs of Giovanni Carlo Affaitadi," who, with a total of 71 shares, held a majority in Antwerp. There were other subsidiaries in Seville, Valladolid, Medina del Campo, Rome, and London. The membership in each one reveals the same interlocking of shareholders.

This structure, similar in many respects to that of a modern holding company, allowed for both a sharing of risks (if a mishap befell one of the companies, it would have only a very limited effect on the others) and a constant supply of fresh capital through the manipulation of shares. The example of the Affaitadi is the only one of which so much is known (the information is provided by their inventory of 1568); but other large Italian and Iberian firms possessed the same organization, which was apparently superior to the other type. Establishing an autonomous subsidiary, detached from the parent company, could enhance the profitability of one branch of the business; this was the case with the

Fuggers' metallurgical interests in the Tyrol and in Carinthia from 1548 on. The same tactic might also serve for purposes of camouflage, as with the company set up in Antwerp in 1546 under a figurehead, in order to exploit the exchange rate differential between Antwerp and Lyons.

Businessmen working alone could also accumulate wealth, although some might occasionally enter into a temporary partnership. At his death in 1597, Simon Ruiz left an estate estimated by his biographer as in the neighborhood of 400,000 florins, as compared to the 500,000 florins that the heirs of Sebastian Neidhart of Augsburg received. The property was of the same magnitude—181,000 Flemish livres, according to the executors' inventory—which went to the heirs of Giovanni Carlo Affaitadi in 1568. (This represented, of course, only a fraction of the Affaitadi "complex.")

Guicciardini assigned to "Seigneur Antoyne [Fugger], who died not long ago in his native land," a personal estate worth "more than 6 million gold écus." We also know, from the balance sheet drawn up after Anton's death, how large a share in the Fugger concern was owned by each of his heirs. An analysis of these figures indicates that a distinction must be made between personal fortunes and the company's assets. A diminution of these assets, as took place with the Fuggers after 1546, can be explained only as the result of the way in which profits were distributed from that date on. Thus, to assert that the Fuggers in 1546 possessed property worth 4.7 million florins (the firm's assets according to the balance sheet), is to introduce a highly misleading statistic.

Besides, the florin of 1597 was worth less than the florin of 1570 and much less than that of 1500. Fortunately we can dispense with calculating the hypothetical rate of depreciation, but one crude fact must be kept in mind: if a person's property, whether estimated in florins, ducats, or écus, ran into six figures, this represented an impressive accumulation of wealth for the sixteenth century. It was a fabulous fortune in the eyes of most men, for whom a hundred or even a few dozen écus constituted a veritable treasure, and, even for many relatively successful businessmen, it represented an enormous sum of money. To round out our picture, we might also mention the sums lost through bankruptcy on the part of a few large firms: the Lippomano bank of Venice in 1499— 140,000 ducats; the Höchstetters in 1529—about 300,000 florins (not to mention all the bankruptcies that occurred everywhere with increasing frequency toward the end of the century, especially in Seville).

In measuring the importance of a businessman by the dimensions of his misfortunes, one is sometimes reminded of his early antecedents. An ancestor of the Paumgartner family, Anton of Nuremberg, went bankrupt in 1465. His son Hans settled in Augsburg, where, from 1498 on, he ranked sixth among the city's taxpayers; the following generation continued this successful climb until, around 1560, they lost almost everything. More often, one has only to go back one or two generations in a businessman's family in order to find a humble personage, whether a simple merchant or an artisan. The world of money, through all the disasters and the triumphs over adversity, was continually renewing itself. On the whole, this process produced more successes than failures, but the mechanisms, the dimensions, and the character of these successes raise a fundamental question for the social historian: what place should one assign the development of the mercantile enterprises of the sixteenth century in the rise of the capitalist system?

THE COMPOSITION OF PROFITS

In order to assert the capitalist character of the big commercial enterprises of the sixteenth century, many historians point to the fact that their supply of capital did not come from accumulated ground rents, but rather from the commercial profits themselves. However, this assertion in itself is not sufficient. One must first determine what constituted the potential sources of profit in the market place. In the gamut of enterprises which we have examined in the preceding pages, the smallest and the largest of these—on the one hand, the shopkeeper and on the other, the big businessman (a capitalist)—do not pose any problems. But where are we to draw the dividing lines?

In reality, the character of the enterprise cannot be understood except when viewed against the panorama of the entire economic system. We would have to know, first of all, the ratio between the volume of exchange and the volume of internal consumption, between domestic production and production for the market. We know this relationship changed and how it changed; we know that this change and its orientation were functions of the increasing division of labor and the development of new technical and social forms of production. But this transformation, whose pace varied from region to region, extended over several centuries—the sixteenth being neither the first nor the last.

Capitalism, in essence, meant the drive for increased profits by means of an increase in volume, earning more by selling more, even if the profit per unit was smaller. This law of the market, despite the multiple correctives that the capitalist forces imposed on the situation, was a crucial factor in the destinies of the industrial concerns of the nineteenth century. By way of contrast, let us recall the conditions prevailing in feudal Europe: a world divided up into a multitude of cells, where the volume of exchange was negligible—minuscule quantities of objects and commodities of very limited usage—though the profits were quite large because of the tremendous costs and risks to the trader.

In the sixteenth century, the profits of businessmen were still, in certain respects, similar to those of the *mercatores* of the late Middle Ages. In the early days of the Portuguese spice trade, certain voyages yielded a profit of 100 percent. In this case, the enormous disparity between cost price and selling price was due, not only to the imperfect state of the lines of communication, but also to the spasmodic, irregular, and embryonic character of the market. Likewise, the financial services rendered to the state produced inflated profits because the risks involved were so great. This was so because a system of public credit was almost totally lacking, whereas nowadays, government bonds are the safest investment for a paterfamilias.

Thus, the most spectacular aspects of what is commonly called, on the basis of a superficial examination of the facts, the "flowering of capitalism in the sixteenth century," attest rather to the fact that, considering the economy in its entirety, the capitalist structures were relatively undeveloped. In the world of everyday commerce, those medium-sized enterprises with their traditional methods (and hence considered "precapitalist") maintained a profit rate that was apparently higher than, for example, that of the companies of south Germany, whose turnovers were infinitely larger. In the latter, we find a more complex structure, more sophisticated methods, far greater capital intensity and gross receipts, but also a lower rate of profit. All this represents whatever was genuinely capitalistic in *Frühkapitalismus*.

THE MERCHANT AND THE PRODUCTION PROCESS

The role played by the sixteenth-century merchants in the transition from domestic production and artisan work to capitalist production was neither exclusive nor absolutely new. The dissociation between capital and labor (a source of antagonism) had already appeared in the thirteenth century, notably in the great textile centers (especially Flanders and Tuscany), but this transformation remained localized. We encounter it again in the sixteenth century, completed in one region, scarcely begun in another, which makes its stages more easily discernible.

The key factor in the first stage was a certain type of delivery contract by which a merchant obtained exclusive disposal of the output of a manufacturer. The exclusiveness was one-sided, for the same buyer could arrange deals with other suppliers, whereas the latter were each obliged to devote all their activity to fulfilling their contracts. For them, this represented the first step toward loss of their independence. The second stage, of far greater consequence, was completed when the buyer advanced the manufacturer a sum of money or when he provided the raw materials. For example, some English merchants in Rouen used this method in order to secure, for a limited period, the entire output of a *cartier* (playing-card manufacturer). In the more essential textile industry, jobbing was the rule.

The evolution was completed when, after a series of loans, the artisan was so in debt to the merchant (or to another manufacturer in the same field or in a field wherein a different operation in the manufacture of the same product was performed) that he pawned his shop and eventually ceded its ownership to his creditor. Examples of the complete triumph of this form of capitalist organization—the "merchant-manufacturer" system—can be found in those industries in England, the Low Countries, and Italy that engaged in heavy exporting. Since there are so few good studies in industrial history that apply the term *capitalism* properly, it is not possible to determine the precise geographical extension of this system. There were several industrial organizations that combined the old and the new; side by side with newly introduced capitalist methods, or even within the framework of a basically capitalistic enterprise, certain structures typical of handicraft production persisted. (They could be found, for example, in a Florentine cloth-making company owned by the Medici.)

Agricultural production did not escape penetration by capital. If the advance of capitalism in this domain was slower and more limited, it was because of the resistance to change offered by the fundamental structures of the rural economy. The merchants took over the development of certain commercial crops. The big merchants of Toulouse made dazzling fortunes in pastel by making the peasants' loans payable, at harvest time, in pastel shells. The development of the plantations in the tropical colonies also constituted direct intervention in production: sugar producers' and slaveholders' capitalism. In the Old World, the exploitation of the land for commercial purposes soon ran into obstacles posed by the demand for subsistence crops. In eastern Europe, however, the abundance of arable land made possible increases in grain production leading to massive exports. The result was a true agrarian capitalism which benefited the nobility but aggravated the misery of the serfs.

Almost everywhere, vast quanitites of land changed hands in the course of the sixteenth century; the merchants bought a great many of them, although they were not the only ones to do so. Often the new proprietor acted in the same way as the old one—more like a *rentier* than an entrepreneur; the explanation for this is to be found in the nature of things rather than in the minds of men.

Actually, there was no fundamental incompatibility between rural interests and mercantile concerns. We have already mentioned some German, Polish, and Danish noblemen functioning as big agricultural entrepreneurs, commanders-in-chief of battalions of serfs. Others emerged as captains of industry: the counts of Mansfeld assumed an active role in the working of their mines and their metallurgical enterprises, in collaboration with some Nuremberg merchants and also a few scholars. In France, more than one squire (*écuyer*—the title that distinguished the true nobleman) living near the coast went to sea in the company of commoners in order to engage in trading. The noble origins of certain German merchant families are not to be questioned, and many Italian merchants had every right to the titles of nobility.

And was not the Church itself, among other things, a moneyed power? This was true, not only of the Curia, but of the missions as well: one could very well call the Jesuit vice-province in Japan a very large capitalist enterprise—no spiritual work without temporal means.

It is necessary to do away with certain simplistic stereotypes, juridical categories, and purely formal distinctions. The image of the nobleman or cleric as a man who did not have the right to engage in commerce and who, moreover, did not concern himself with questions of money, belongs in the museum of obsolete historiography. The business world knew no such restrictions.

EDUCATION

Not even the smallest trader could get along without knowing how to count, but did he know how to read and write? Very frequently he did, without a doubt: there are few crosses at the bottom of notarial documents signed by very humble merchants. As soon as a man began conducting business in a foreign country, he faced the problem of languages as well as that of correspondence. Of course, the Breton who frequented the ports of the Low Countries or the Fleming who came to France could easily find an interpreter in innkeepers or compatriots who had settled there. But then there was the Dutch shipmaster, Martin Martin, who in 1576 placed his son in the home of one Jehan Lambert, called "the Fleming," a merchant living near Rouen, so that the boy could go to school to learn French. This is admittedly a very tiny detail, and, what is more, the métier of a seaman (a modest social status) was particularly conducive to an interest in languages, but this glimpse of the school gives this anecdote a somewhat broader significance.

There is very good reason to believe that in the towns of the sixteenth century, rudimentary education was provided on a fairly large scale, either through private instructors or community schools. We know of a municipal ordinance, dealing with the community schools in Zwickau (in Saxony), that recommended that certain students be selected who would be capable of learning Latin, while the others would pursue their studies no further. The issue here was promotion from the first to the second educational level. Another glimpse of the situation is provided by a chronicler who relates that in 1481, Emperor Frederick III, on arriving in Nuremberg, was greeted by four thousand youngsters led by their schoolmasters and schoolmistresses. These tidbits of information, although unconfirmed, have some basis in fact. It is known that as early as the thirteenth century, there were lay schools in Italy that prepared the future merchant for his apprenticeship.

The contents of this first level of instruction was based on practical considerations. Once the child had mastered the rudiments of reading, he was given texts which taught him all that he had to know about the calendar and provided him with a basic commercial vocabulary (types of cloth, weights and measures, coin names). All the lessons were seasoned with a bit of moral instruction in the form of a catechism, which took the place of more formal religious instruction. Handwriting instruction reflected the same practical concerns. Certain formularies, which have been preserved—veritable handbooks of handwriting—clearly had a dual purpose. The space devoted to proper lettering, and even ornamentation, betrays a devotion to esthetic standards that must have exceeded the calligraphic capacities of even the most advanced students. Thus, one aspect was an emphasis on "art for art's sake" virtuosity, as can be seen from the following title: "A good handbook and brief instruction manual containing the excellent principles by which those youths desirous of writing elegantly may be taught and drilled with remarkable art and with rapidity, written by Johannes Neudorffer, burgher and arithmetic teacher of Nuremberg, compiled so as to make them more readily comprehensible to his students, in the year of our Lord and Savior Jesus Christ MDXXXVIII. Nulla dies signe linea." The author, a friend of Dürer, was a very famous teacher in his time, the leader of his own school, as it were, who trained many disciples. But the content of these calligraphed texts was also instructive, for they taught the student how to compose a letter and the proper turns of phrase. He was thus initiated into the ways of commerce.

The teaching of arithmetic was the very next step. Elementary education did not always cover the four basic operations. The child first learned to "cipher," that is, to read and write numbers and, at the same time, was taught the current system of weights and measures, the metric system of those days. The contract of a schoolmaster, engaged by a small German town in 1544, fixed the fees that the students were to pay in order to learn how to read and write; for those who wanted, in addition, to learn how to count and to write a clerkly hand, the rates were to be negotiated by the master and the parents. The fundamentals of arithmetic were given only after two or three years of study, when, as the Italians phrased it, the student moved on to the abacus. This German schoolmaster's textbooks, some of which have come down to us, were for the most part handwritten. However, there were some printed treatises on arithmetic, and most of them went through a considerable number of editions: *The Abacus* of Pietro Borgi, for example, was first published in Venice in 1484 and, in less than one hundred years' time, was reprinted sixteen times.

Was this arithmetic for schoolchildren or for more knowledgeable readers, for an adult audience? Sometimes an author states explicitly that his book was designed for youngsters; thus, the title of Adam Rise's book (first edition published in Erfurt in 1518) read: "Little book of arithmetic, for teaching children the fundamentals of counting, and leading them to the comprehension of larger things." The claims made in prefaces should not be taken too literally since every author would praise the superior qualities of his own work, and each new edition was, as a rule, enriched by "a few new rules, fine and profitable"—even if the whole thing was a plagiary from beginning to end. Often, very little erudition was displayed.

A few works, however, had some real scientific value; they were probably utilized more by vulgarizers who had a fair grasp of their contents or by very experienced merchants than by students and apprentices. The *Summa de Arithmetica Geometrica Proportioni et Proportionalita* by the Franciscan Luca Pacioli, printed in Venice in 1494, is the prime example of these works, being both a compendium of mathematics and an encyclopedia of commerce. More typical in a sense, although far less substantial, was the short treatise in Latin by Gemma Frisius, published in Wittenberg in 1542; the examples and the exercises in the book did not represent a system of commercial practices but rather was designed for the university student. Scholars with credentials as authentic as those of Gemma Frisius carried on in the tradition of Pacioli. Cardan, Tartaglia, Stevin, for example, all devoted chapters or whole sections of their treatises on mathematics to commercial practice and especially to bookkeeping. Moreover, these treatises were not merely didactic, they also contributed to the advancement of knowledge.

On a much lower level, the mere arithmeticians furnished the merchants with material that was plainly more utilitarian. Valentin Mennher said as much in rather blunt language. The author of a treatise on bookkeeping (published in French and German) which not only lacked originality, but in which bookkeeping was treated only briefly in an appendix to what amounted to an arithmetic primer, he sought to improve his own standing by denigrating those who, "without having observed or exercised the conduct of merchandising . . . through lack of experience, have put forward examples of little benefit." Books on commercial arithmetic dealt first with numeration and the "four principal rules of Arithmetic which are Adding, Subtracting, Multiplying, and Dividing broken as well as whole numbers," and then quickly went on to practical problems such as "the reduction of coins," metrological conversions, alloy proportions, and the computation of prices, interest, and exchange rates. The reader was given formulas, of which the "ell chart" offers an excellent illustration. "Broken numbers" no doubt caused many people tremendous difficulty; hence, they preferred a roundabout approach with concrete examples, and not even those authors who had carefully explained the addition of fractions and mixed numbers considered such an exposition superfluous. The reader was usually given formulas, of which the ell* chart is an excellent illustration.

Jean Trenchant explained the matter thus: "Some add fractions differently, especially fractions of an ell by the parts of a franc or 20 s. [sous]. Let us suppose they wanted to add 1/2, 2/3, 1/4, 5/6, 3/8, and 7/12 ells. First, for 1/2, they put down 10 s. which is one half of a franc, for 2/3 they put down 13s. 4 den. [deniers], for 1/4 5 s., and so on" (the total being 3 livres 4 sous 2 deniers or 3 and 5/24 ells). A chart in a book spared the merchant the trouble of doing all the calculations. Like their readers, the authors themselves often displayed a marked incapacity for

*An old measurement of length, especially used for cloth, varying from 27 to 45 inches.

handling abstract notions. This is how Mennher presents the idea of compound interest: "A merchant borrows some money at 12 percent interest per year and lends the same money at one percent per month, the question being if one adds up the profit made each month, how much will his profit be at the end of the year . . ."—whereupon Mennher solves the problem by addition!

One can perceive immediately the difference in intellectual levels when one reads a passage like the following from Trenchant: "Money which earns interest at the end of a term increases by a geometric progression: therefore, all the following questions will be resolved by means of this rule." And, in fact, Trenchant, employing this rule, then proceeds to calculate an annuity of the Grand Parti, just as it should be done. His book was not written for beginners.

Over and above these important differences, one essential characteristic was common to all works on commercial arithmetic: they all contained rules that derived more from the art of merchandising than from the science of numbers—and sometimes there was even a "brief disquisition on monetary exchange." The young man taking up the study of bookkeeping no doubt found it necessary to digest the simplest of such treatises. Having just turned fourteen, Lucas Rem, accompanied by the Welsers' factors, left Augsburg for Venice, where he was to get an education. There, within the space of five and one-half months, he learned how to do sums (he might already have known how to cipher in German) and then went on to learn bookkeeping, which did not take him more than three months. The teaching of bookkeeping was, in effect, the highest level of business instruction. At the beginning of the sixteenth century, Venice enjoyed a unique reputation throughout the world in this regard; other centers arose in Nuremberg, Lyons, and, most notably, Antwerp, but the primacy of Venice was not shaken. We shall consider the nature of bookkeeping later on, examining both the precepts and their practical application. But, as we follow Lucas Rem in his studies, our attention is now drawn to one final aspect of the merchant's formal training—foreign languages.

Before beginning the study of arithmetic under a German tutor in Venice, Rem spent eighteen months with two Italian teachers in order to learn the language. Subsequently, still following the Welser itinerary, he traveled to Lyons, but before becoming their factor there, he spent a year learning French with a local schoolmaster, of whom he retained some unpleasant memories. The pedagogue's wife was so stingy that the boarders were compelled to pilfer their food and wine from her. Thus, at the age of eighteen, before having really entered upon his career, Rem had mastered two foreign languages. His training had been particularly thorough, more so, perhaps, than the average merchant's, but a great many merchants were polyglot. If Gian Carlo Affaitadi could spend forty years of his life in the Low Countries without hardly ever using any language but Italian, it was because the Italians in the sixteenth century were in the same position as the English-speaking people today. Their language was the international language of business, except in the region stretching from the Low Countries to the edge of the Slavic world, where the principal language was Low German. In the latter area, the language barrier was more difficult to overcome and interpreters were very valuable people—especially to the merchants coming from very far away (in Reval, young employees had to learn Russian as part of their apprenticeship). To many historians, a major consequence of the economic importance achieved by the Low Countries, a bilingual region, was the diffusion of the French language toward the east and the north; just as the importance of Lyons prompted the ambitious merchants of south Germany to learn French, a *welche* (non-Teutonic and hence truly foreign) language.

In Europe's Atlantic regions, the French language benefited from France's intermediate (geographical, if not linguistic) position between Seville or Lisbon and Amsterdam or Danzig; hence, French was soon second only to Italian, despite the spread of Spanish and English. Generally speaking, for their training, or at least for the finishing touches, young people traveled westward or southward. But the traffic was not all one way. Spaniards came to France and Frenchmen went to Spain.

In 1533, Friedrich Behaim of Nuremberg, who, in 1506, at the age of fifteen, had gone to Lyons to learn the trade, sent his son Paul to Cracow (the boy would later become a factor for the Imhofs at Antwerp). He placed his son in the hands of the representatives of the Florentine firm of Pietro Antonio de Nobili. This was the crucial stage in his training: going to work for an established firm.

PROCEDURES

The proliferation of books written for the edification of merchants suggests that they enjoyed a certain popularity, but the merchants themselves almost never spoke about them. On the other hand, we know that once an enterprise reached a certain size, its operation required the compilation and preservation of data and documents, which were no doubt used in training apprentices but were not destined to be made public. Such was *Procedures*, the prototype of which had been the *Pratica della Mercatura*, written by the fourteenth-century Florentine, Francesco Balducci Pegolotti. A series of manuscripts belonging to the Paumgartners of Augsburg and composed between 1480 and 1540, *Procedures* constitutes the most voluminous collection that has come down to us. In the opinion of the compilers, it contains all the knowledge needed to conduct business in those trading towns with which the firm maintained relations: metrological and monetary information, taxes to be paid and various regulations, and finally, information of a "technological" character (qualities and peculiarities of various commodities). In all, an enormous catalogue, but one limited to the markets and types of business in which the firm was involved. The Paumgartners were hardly concerned at all with the northern and eastern parts of Europe.

One of the manuscripts was devoted to colonial commerce; in form, it resembles a geographical dissertation:

Pearls
In the Indies there are two places where the best pearls are to be seen. And, in the Persian Sea not far from Ormuz, one finds more pearls than

anywhere else. Ormuz is an island one mile from the mainland and has its own king, who is a follower of Mohammed. . . . Djeddah is a city on the Red Sea and a port to which come all the ships laden with spices which come from the Indies, and the city is called the port of Mecca, because these ships cannot go any further inland. And it is there that all the spices must be loaded in small boats called *galbess* and carried in this fashion as far as the gorge at the foot of Mount Sinai and then borne by camels to Cairo and Alexandria.

Elsewhere can be found the details of a shipment of almonds and cumin from Bari to Antwerp, with all the figures for each facet of the operation; this is certainly not an imaginary schema. There are a few pages that provide a brief but pertinent summary of monetary exchange. This matter is also discussed with particular reference to certain trading towns—one section, for example, is entitled "Lyons." When first written, these sections were lacking in clarity, as shown by the fact that in 1527, Hans Paumgartner added a model draft in Italian, in his own hand, to the above-mentioned passage, which had been composed years earlier. The tool was reworked as need dictated and gradually perfected through the addition of new information.

Thus, by going about his daily tasks, the apprentice learned merchandising, a practical art. An apprenticeship in a shop was for the most part much simpler than one in a firm which, by 1515, knew all there was to know about trading in the East Indies or the methods of defrauding the King in Lisbon. But even medium-sized enterprises utilized manuals which, though reflecting their more limited horizons, were in all essential respects like those used by the big firms. Around the year 1560, fifteen-year-old Jakob Stöve of Munster, an employee of a Danzig tradesman, prepared a notebook in which he marked down pertinent data concerning certain commodities, weights and measures, coins, and various itineraries, including the distances between cities. This no doubt represented all that he had to know—and perhaps also all that went on in his master's business.

From the end of·the fifteenth century on, in Italy (somewhat later elsewhere) the development of printing led to the publication of works based on private procedures. There was thus a series of Italian price lists, and in 1548, the *Handelbuch* of Lorenz Meder was published in Nuremberg. Although the mere idea of imparting such data to the general public met with some resistance, the fact remains that the information had already been, to a small extent, taught by the arithmeticians and, in part, had become public domain. The important thing is that once they were printed in book form, their presentation became systematic—and eventually truly encyclopedic. From this point of view, Meder's book was of very limited applicability, since it did not cover all the material currently available. Even more than this limitation, it was full of dry facts. The book typifies the outlook of the entire training given the apprentice merchant; it contained no mathematics or geography or jurisprudence in the truly academic sense, but instead a little of everything reduced to the level of a guide or handbook.

However, one can appreciate the value of such an education, if one considers the state of scientific knowledge in the sixteenth century: petrified drivel, impervious to whatever was going on in the world. Some very weighty tomes, published in 1540 and even later, still failed to mention the discovery of America in their descriptions of the world. Men of action had no use for abstract learning; their knowledge, crude and empirical, was always subordinated to the superiority of experience. The merchant was a man who was constantly recording very specialized data, a man who accumulated varied experiences. We have already observed Lucas Rem in Lyons in 1495; in 1503, in Saragossa, he was "learning a great deal about the wool trade," and on his first trip to Antwerp in 1508, he tarried there for a month and a half, once again "in order to learn." There was no trace of method in all this, but simply the idea that education continued at any age, in any place, and with the joy of discovery and travel. A merchant from Nuremberg, newly settled in Cracow, explained his perpetual peregrinations as follows: "I am very glad that I do not have to remain always in the same town; indeed, he who remains always in the same town learns but little." By the terms of that contract concluded at La Rochelle which we analyzed earlier (Chapter IV), Bouet was to take his servant along "so as to give him an opportunity to learn and to see distant lands." This open-mindedness was one of the most characteristic features of the merchant mentality.

VIII

Behind the Counter and on the Road

Commerce involved certain physical operations, namely, handling and shipping, which were not performed by the merchant nor, for that matter, by his factors or his shop assistants. Every town had its army of mechanical auxiliaries—packers, porters, carters, dockers—who were organized into groups independent of the commercial enterprises. One could not do without their services. Even the biggest merchants did not have laborers qualified to carry out these tasks. Manual labor was no part of the art of merchandising. This art was exclusively concerned with negotiating—palavering—a term which covers a number of diverse activities.

On the basis of some rare documents, G. Mickwitz has been able to reconstruct the entire work schedule for the year 1549, of Tönnis Smidt, an average merchant from Reval. Here, for example, is what transpired during the month of March: Few purchases made. This is the month when merchandise purchased earlier arrives, and preparations are being made in anticipation of the resumption of ocean travel with the coming of spring. On March 1, four shipments of flax from Narva are brought in on sleds; their total weight falls short of the amount he contracted for. Hence, Smidt withholds a portion of the sum due the carriers; they will be reimbursed by the shipper in Narva if they were not responsible for the shortage. In addition, Smidt sends back whatever flax of inferior quality the shipment may contain. On March 15, he receives 4,000 calfskins, which will be stored in the cellar, and four more shipments of flax, which include the remainder of the previous order and that purchased in a separate transaction. On the 16th, payment is received for furs sold in February; on the 20th, flax purchased on February 12 is sold. Eventually, the flax is brought to the weighing machine, barrels and nails are purchased, the flax is packed in these barrels.

Large-scale international commerce thus on the whole appears as an endless succession of rather restricted activities, with the merchant running back and forth between his cellars, attics, sheds, and "counter," that is, his office (usually located in the main hall, though sometimes in a special room), where he kept his books, papers, and money locked up in a closet and in strong-boxes. As for the factor stationed in a foreign country, if his master lacked the means to buy or rent him a house, he would work in an inn, storing his goods in vast coach-houses furnished by the innkeeper (unless the municipal authorities placed a public building at the merchants' disposal to serve as a warehouse for various types of commodities). If this factor happened to be in a town where he and his fellow nationals were, more or less, forced to live in one particular place, as in the Fondaco of Venice, his existence strongly resembled that in a barracks. There is a document dating from 1508 that lists the tenants of the Fondaco's seventy-six rooms: the representatives of each of the largest firms occupied two rooms—the Fuggers were in rooms 1 and 2 on the prestigious second *(Sopra Canal Grande)* floor, the Welsers in rooms 23 and 24 on the next floor. The document also indicated the distribution of the twenty-five *"magazeni."*

In the medium-sized enterprise, there was neither a cashier nor a secretary; their functions were discharged by the merchant himself. Besides, conducting his own correspondence made it easier to maintain secrecy in his business dealings. A compatriot of Tönnis Smidt wrote such a poor hand that he had to have his letters recopied. This caused him some grief, as he noted in 1532: "I did not learn enough in my youth, and that vexes me." He was an exception perhaps, but the fact was that there were numerous merchants whose handwriting left something to be desired. As for the account books, although simple in principle, they were actually rather complicated affairs, precisely because of their unmethodical character; this confusion appears all the greater when contrasted with the advantages of double-entry bookkeeping.

Before taking up this comparison, however, it might be advisable to describe the setting, the personnel, and the working conditions in a large enterprise. Working with the chief at headquarters or with the factor in a branch office was a small number of top-level employees who either served as amanuenses or carried out their superior's commands, exercising in this capacity a variable amount of personal initiative. The Welsers' foreign trading office at Lisbon had anywhere from three to six employees between 1503 and 1508—a rather large staff; Simon Ruiz never assigned more than three to an office at any one time. In the largest companies there was a more complex division of labor. The Bonvisi firm of Lyons, in addition to the two directors, had two or three proxies who, on being appointed, sent their signatures to the firm's correspondents. The Fugger company displayed a particularly high degree of organization. In the "golden chamber," Jakob maintained a veritable general staff, which included a proxy to handle lawsuits and a chief bookkeeper, Matthäus Schwarz, who had other bookkeepers under his command, each of whom audited the accounts of one or more foreign trading offices. In 1592, according to the records, there was even an archivist. Incoming correspondence and copies of letters sent out were methodically filed in pigeonholes, whereas with businessmen who lacked such equipment, papers were not kept in any particular order. In most cases, the fixtures consisted of little more than one or two writing desks with writing kits, an exchequer and counters for computations, and a balance scale for testing coins (identical to the one that was included in the standard equipment of the money changer). Much more unusual, no doubt, was the address book used around 1540 by Anton Fugger's secretaries; an item usually found in chancelleries, it contained a list of royal titles, the purpose being to avoid blunders when composing letters to sovereigns. But, in every business, the work was almost always the same.

Except for a break to attend mass, wrote André Ruiz from Nantes in 1576, in a letter to his brother Simon, "it is writing letters and more letters all day long." As if echoing him, Balthazar Paumgartner wrote to his wife from Augsburg in 1584: "You know that, during the winter, I must spend many hours in the office after dark." Correspondence was the very heart of any firm engaged in international commerce. With Italian companies, a sharp line was drawn between, on the one hand, letters concerning current business, which dealt with purchases, sales, or shipments of goods or contained financial statements or the current prices on the commodities and money markets, and on the other hand, private letters bearing political and commercial news, which were considered strictly confidential and were not to be read by any employee. The constricting and unpleasant nature of work in the shop, together with the patriarchal atmosphere (the employees, provided with room and board, had to take their meals with the master), proved more than young, adventurous spirits could bear. H.U. Krafft left H. Imhof in 1572 after ten years of service; he had found his sojourns in Lyons and Florence more enjoyable than keeping the books in Augsburg. He then joined the Manlichs, who sent him on trips, until the firm's bankruptcy landed him in a Syrian prison. Indeed, it was necessary for part of the staff to travel—in particular, the young masters, who went to study at first hand the operating procedures of the establishments they would eventually be directing from afar. While Jakob was still alive, Anton Fugger worked in Rome, Breslau, and Cracow, but, neither during this period nor subsequently, did he ever travel to Antwerp. Generally speaking, factors could not really complain that their life was too sedentary. Even if they had to stay at one post for a long time, the scope of their responsibilities forced them to engage in a wide variety of activities. In 1511, Lucas Rem was serving as the Welsers' factor in Antwerp, assisted by only one colleague—and only intermittently at that—he was obliged to attend the fairs at Berg, Middelburg, and sometimes Bruges, and often had to go to the Court. In addition, he was responsible for keeping the books, his most important and most time consuming chore. In the absence of a trained bookkeeper, only an experienced employee who inspired absolute confidence or if need be, the chief himself (as in Rem's case), could be entrusted with this task.

THE ART OF ACCOUNTING

The merchants' most jealously guarded secrets were all hidden in their account books. Any attempts by the authorities to examine a merchant's books—even when there were valid judicial reasons for doing so—aroused sharp reaction. The function and the importance of bookkeeping in any enterprise varied considerably, depending on the bookkeeping system employed, so these methods are of more than technical interest.

For the majority of ordinary merchants, bookkeeping had two limited objectives. We have already noted that payments in cash were rare, the creditor taking promissory notes from his debtors instead, but a small piece of paper could easily be mislaid. In its most rudimentary and most widespread form, bookkeeping consisted of making a note of any transactions involving credit; the account book in this case was simply a chronological record, serving as a memory aid. (If the merchant also entered his domestic expenses and the events of his family life, his day-book could hardly be distinguished from a family record book.) In some cases the arrangement was somewhat more systematic, one debtor to a page, for example; this allowed the merchant to indicate receipt of payment on the opposite page, if he was not content merely to cross out the first entry.

The other purpose that simple bookkeeping was originally intended to serve arose when partnerships were formed with distant merchants. Robert Bouchard of Carentan and Jehan Leger til of Rouen, upon forming a partnership, agreed to "keep a daily record" of their purchases and sales. Similarly, the companies of the Hanseatic merchants maintained "books of merchandise." Each partner would mark down all the goods he received from the other, as well as the shipping costs paid on delivery and the selling price. Settling accounts was accomplished by comparing the entries in one partner's book with those in the other's—a comparison that took place through the mail. Needless to say, this took an enormous amount of time, and, very often, accounts were never settled unless the death of one of the contracting parties compelled the other to straighten things out with the executors of the deceased's will. There was another obvious disadvantage to this system: it did not encompass all of a merchant's transactions; even after this system had been improved, it did not show the merchant where he stood as far as his own business was concerned. Certain rather clever modifications, designed to facilitate the calculation of profits and losses, attest to the indirect influence of the advances associated with the spread of the superior technique of double-entry bookkeeping, an Italian invention which was no longer new. The basic idea of double-entry was that every transaction entailed two separate entries in the *Big Book*; what was credited to one account had to be debited to another. The starting point was still the day-book. Classifying the various types of accounts and determining their interconnections posed some problems that not every large enterprise was able to solve as skillfully as the Italian masters. But no matter how great the differences on the technical level, the fact remained that by applying the double-entry principle, a firm was able to maintain a constant check and to detect any errors or omissions. Hence, if it was not always possible to draw up a true balance sheet, one could at least follow, with sufficient precision, one's financial progress through the reckoning of profits and losses.

Long a secret of the Italians, in the sixteenth century double-entry bookkeeping was adopted by merchants in other countries. Very few account books kept in this fashion from the Low Countries, Spain, and Germany have been preserved, but the large number of extant bookkeeping manuals is another form of proof. Some of them display an originality that bears witness to the great strides made by bookkeeping theory; and all of them—even those that were merely skillfully plagiarized from earlier works—reflect the advent of a new course in arithmetic taught by masters who were familiar with "accountancy in the Italian manner." Thus, there was increased public interest, as well as an increase in the number of trained bookkeepers.

If the authors' boastings for publicity purposes are ignored, one can see how far this new, superior technique had spread, emanating, not only from Venice, but by this time from Antwerp as well. When in 1581, a Danzig schoolmaster, Sebastian Gammersfelder of Passau, answered his critics' charge that his treatise published in 1570 was a plagiary, he asserted that they were "no more capable of judging bookkeeping than was a cow of judging a new church portal." He may well have been right; for many people the subject was a complete mystery. Still, all over Europe the progress achieved in this field was great enough to render obsolete a project which, it seems, Matthäus Schwarz, a few decades earlier, had hoped would bring him glory. Jakob Fugger's chief bookkeeper had, in fact, composed for the instruction of young people, a brief dissertation on his art, to which he had appended a specimen page taken directly from the firm's records—namely, the accounts of the Venetian foreign trading office for the year 1516. Perhaps because of the model's close resemblance to reality, his master vetoed the whole idea, thus depriving him of the pleasure of seeing his work published. For us, this manuscript is especially precious, since all of the Fuggers' books have been lost. At that time, the technique employed in their firm was not Italian double-entry, yet, in a remarkable fashion, the accounts of one foreign trading office could be used to check those of another, as witness this note written by Schwarz himself on January 6, 1524: "On this day, I have written to Christoph Muelich and Hans Fugger in Rome that in Rome's accounts, under the heading, Paid 20 April 1520, the following appears: 45 ducats to Christoph de Schnitingen for draft of 8 March on Nuremberg; and under Paid 15 September 1520, 21 ducats to Valentin Thetenloh for draft of 27 July on Nuremberg. Neither of these drafts has been entered in Nuremberg's books. They are to send copies of the drafts to me, here in Augsburg."

TRAVELING

The obstacles and the perils that the men of this period faced were attributable not only to the schemes of commercial rivals, but, above all, to nature. Nothing illustrates this better than the hazards of transportation. One should not be misled by the expression "sedentary merchant," rightly used only to distinguish international commerce "in the Italian style" from the caravan trade. In the sixteenth century, the merchant was of necessity a traveling man, and it never occurred to him to bemoan this fact. This applied not only to the small tradesmen on their way to the fairs, but also to top-level employees and sometimes to the very masters of the most powerful enterprises. Let us rejoin Lucas Rem during his years at Lyons. Here is a summary of his travels:

    1500   Lyons–Bourges–Paris–Rouen–Lyons
           Lyons–Albi–Lyons
           Lyons–Switzerland–Lyons
    1501   Lyons–Augsburg–Lyons
           Lyons–Switzerland–Lyons
    1502   Lyons–Switzerland–Lyons
           Lyons–Augsburg–Lyons
           Lyons–Albi–Lyons
           Lyons–Toulouse–Saragossa

(In 1503, he took up his new post in Lisbon.)

After Lisbon, where he was in charge, he traveled to Morocco, Madeira, the Azores, and the Cape Verde Islands. The merchant was, of course, a man of the pen, but he was equally familiar with the horse. The wretched condition of the roads, if they existed at all, hindered his movements, especially during the winter months. But the traveler had other enemies beside the wind and the cold: robber barons (the breed was not yet extinct); troops of soldiers (sometimes enrolled in the service of a prince), in an age when peace was rare; and, finally, more than anything, the ubiquitous bandits (the subject of a study by Fernand

Braudel). The very real risk of being robbed did not stop the merchant from using the highways, but the historian must nevertheless take these dangers into account, while avoiding the pitfall of mistaking the occasional occurrence for history.

The historian must pay even closer attention to the other factors contributing to the precariousness of communications: for example, the delays and irregularity of mail deliveries, despite the first feeble attempts at postal organization. Royal or imperial post, municipal couriers, special delivery for important occasions—every form of postal service was risky. In 1568, Simon Ruiz's correspondent at Rouen sent out three copies of the same letter, one via Nantes, the second via Paris, and the last by sea. As far as the conveyance of goods was concerned, the situation was even worse. There were many hauling companies servicing the essential trade routes: for thirty-five years, a company of Milanese carters "conducted" goods between Antwerp and Italy. In Germany, the Hessians were veritable transporting specialists, well known in Antwerp. This traffic, which was not immune to plundering raids, suffered more than a mere horseback rider would from the inconveniences caused by bad weather. Hence, the waterways were used as much as possible, and if rivers were treacherous, "the perils and chances of the sea" were even more so. This topic is so vast that we must confine ourselves to those aspects of it that directly affected the practice of merchandising, although, in these matters, nothing escaped the attention of the businessman.

COMMERCE AND MARITIME SHIPPING

The sixteenth century witnessed an increasing separation between strictly commercial interests and shipping interests. The distinction between the two was due to an inescapable fact: when the merchant traveled with his merchandise, it was not he who commanded the ship, even though his presence on board was an element in the system, whereby the technical functions of the navigator were markedly counterbalanced by the merchant's commercial functions. This equilibrium was

destroyed as soon as their partnership was replaced by a contract between the transporter and the charterer. However, the first type of
relationship did not disappear entirely in the sixteenth century. A certain number of men would unite for the purpose of outfitting a ship that
they had bought or built, having "shared the costs and expenses," and
reserving one share for the captain of their choice. They would load the
ship with merchandise to be sold for their account at the destination.
To facilitate the sale of these goods and the purchase of cargo for the
return trip, one or more members of the *parsonnerie* would go along,
since the captain could not perform all these tasks by himself.

This system of freighting contracts or "charter parties" made things
easier. The shipmaster, in the name of the "bourgeois" (owners) (unless
he himself were the bourgeois "sole owner") undertook to make a
voyage, usually roundtrip, following a predetermined route, for the account of one or several merchants. Their mutual obligations were set
down in great detail. Nothing prevented the merchants from owning
their own fleet, of course. The merchants of the Hanse and of La
Rochelle often owned shares in ships, one-fourth of this vessel or one-
eighth of that vessel. But the biggest firms, as a rule, did without. The
Coral Company at Marseilles owned only two ships, and, whenever
necessary, would resort to chartering. A charter party engaged two
juridically equal parties. Theoretically, shipping could have proved as
lucrative an enterprise as commerce—after all, the maritime companies
of our day are no less powerful than their clients—but the fact of the
matter is that in the sixteenth century, the situation was entirely different.

Despite his absolute authority over the crew, the shipmaster (in effect,
a mere technical specialist) found himself in a situation more like that
of his men than that of a businessman. The charterer, fearing treachery
on the transporter's part, imposed a multitude of restrictions and
abridged his right of "portage," the trading that he could conduct for
his own account, which sometimes enabled him to become a merchant
in his own right. There were also the bourgeois, often individuals of

modest means, who took part in transporting merchandise and inhabited the towns around the great seaports; they hardly seem worthy of the name of skippers. An important exception must be made for those whose principal occupation was privateering, such as Ango from Dieppe or certain Englishmen. These men were also merchants, of course, since they had booty to sell. In this sense, the tradition exemplified by Ango remains intact; since the king always had enemies, a business voyage could always be livened up with some profitable diversion. Privateering never disappeared entirely from the maritime scene, but the biggest businessmen generally left such enterprises to others (unless, as in England or Holland, privateering took on a political character in the service of the national cause). Their timidity in this regard was owing to the high-risk character of the profits—whoever assaulted others was in danger of being assaulted himself. In 1531, Ango himself chose to bargain with the Portuguese, against whom he had obtained a "letter of marque" for 250,000 ducats, rather than use this royal document which authorized him to conduct raids on their ships; he no doubt made a handsomer profit by negotiating.

Many merchants did not wish to incorporate maritime transport into their business operations. Such a pursuit would have been too different from their own work, and technical considerations made them reluctant to burden themselves with a new set of problems. Naval history recorded a great many advances between the fifteenth and seventeenth centuries, but, in many respects, these advances were inconsequential. Men were traveling all the way to America and the Indies, but as far as voyages between Italy and the Near East or between the Low Countries and Spain were concerned, there was hardly any improvement from the standpoint of regularity or security. Navigators had successfully defied the sea, but they had not mastered her. Let us return to the above-mentioned advances.

Ships, no doubt, were larger than before but the question of size is a complicated one and in the end, experts cannot say for sure what was meant by "caravel" or "galleon." In any case, for a number of reasons, the maximum size was quickly reached. First of all, port installations were still primitive, and the largest ports were often on rivers and therefore, difficult of access (as was the case with Antwerp, Rouen, and Seville). Secondly, the seaworthiness of ships having large tonnages was dubious; the heavy ships used on the Mediterranean were hardly fit for sailing the Atlantic. Here, the medium-sized sailing ship, which was generally closer to one hundred than to two hundred tons, proved its superiority. The more spacious vessels, even if they handled well on the high seas, still had certain drawbacks. Very understandably, merchants did not want to risk everything on one voyage. Had navigation gained in reliability? Of course, the conquest of the Atlantic represented a tremendous advance. The successes of Christopher Columbus and Vasco da Gama marked the definitive establishment of routes that were almost perfect, as regards winds and currents, but the trade winds do not blow in Europe, where the instability of the weather made forecasting virtually impossible. Men knew how to deal with heavy weather and maneuver against the wind, but still there had to be a wind for the ship to leave harbor. As for the revolution (long under way) in rudder design, the constant improvement of the keels, and the advances in the deployment of the sails, we must leave it to the experts to decide which played the leading role.

But it is the result that counts the most—the days and weeks wasted while waiting for "the first spell of favorable weather that it will please God to send," the ships bound for the Low Countries ending up near the coast of Ireland, and, then, the shipwrecks—these were the hazards of the sea. After a certain degree of frequency is reached, accidents are regarded as part of the natural order. Not that navigators sailed blind; maps and instruments were being used more and more, and for voyages in unfamiliar waters, a "cosmograph" was invariably taken on board. If they had kept abreast of the most recent discoveries of nautical science, they could determine a ship's latitude fairly easily, although the determination of longitude was far more difficult, since they lacked good instruments for telling time. In the trial analysis, they simply navigated by dead reckoning. Every voyage proved a perilous adventure, even when the distance was not very great and the route was familiar.

The uncertainty of communications and transportation, which can be compared with the uncertain character of the harvests that determined the rhythm of economic life, represented the principal element of risk in the merchant's activities. We can thus perceive the two poles between which the business world oscillated: on the one hand, steady improvements in organization and the rationalization of technique and, on the other hand, the resistance offered by an unpredictable reality, still irrational and chaotic, considering the means of action at man's disposal. This contrast is one of the keys to understanding the merchant's mental universe.

sales depending entirely on a wager. One day in July 1502, Johann Lambersen wagered that the Duke of Guelderland had already captured the castle to which his troops were laying siege; Arnt von Emmerich took the opposite position. The deal was as follows: If, by the date of the bet, the Duke had in fact succeeded, Emmerich would pay Lambersen 420 florins (an exorbitant price) for three bags or about one hundred pounds of saffron; if not, Emmerich would receive the saffron gratis. A deal concluded in 1534 was based on an even stranger stipulation (which, by the way, caused it to be legally annulled): the deal would go through on condition that the seller marry a nun or a nun's daughter. He kept his part of the bargain, but the buyer found a loophole.

It is true that the bizarre nature of such agreements often concealed a usurious intent, but one should not consider this aspect alone. These arrangements represented an archaic, and hence less abstract, form of speculation, which consisted of selling merchandise at the price it would have at a later date. In principle, such an operation was no different from what we call speculation today, namely, the systematic purchase and stocking of goods with a view to profiting from variations in the market price. In this case, the outcome of the wager depends on the economic conditions and not on some fortuitous event coming to pass—an important difference; but the "betting" psychology is the same in both cases. The gambling mania that existed in the great financial centers resulted in a proliferation of lotteries as well as wagers—betting on the rates of exchange or the sex of unborn children. In the second case, the payoff was made upon receipt of a "letter of parturition"; occasionally, this led to fraud, as happened in Antwerp and Medina del Campo, whenever the mother could be bought off by one of the parties and persuaded to hide her newborn child for a few days. Considering the riskiness of many short-term commercial operations, it was just as much chance in both business and gambling that picked the winners. One could be more assured of success if one gave chance a little help by cheating in gambling or by being clever in business (the latter quality might even be called a virtue). And how should the organizers of lotteries be classified?

"Lottery dupery," wrote one citizen of Antwerp as he signed the lottery ticket—but he signed up nonetheless. There would be no sense in dwelling on the various methods of exploiting the gullible public, if they did not represent—in their own uncommendable way—a victory for that spirit of organization which is part and parcel of the business world.

On a more general level, the development of insurance was part of the same movement, the same effort to eliminate the baneful effects of chance. Two centuries earlier, the Italians, soon followed by the Iberians, had perfected maritime insurance against the hazards of sea travel; the idea spread to the western and northern parts of Europe in the sixteenth century, without entirely replacing the older, more primitive system of high-risk loans (to which, as we have seen, Claude Daubray resorted in 1576). The high interest on these loans included an insurance premium; if the borrower returned safely to port, he rarely paid less than 20 percent on an ordinary voyage and up to 50 percent on a voyage to America. In the event of a shipwreck, the lender lost his capital.

Furnishing insurance was one of the most common forms of investment for the big businessman. However, insurance lent itself easily to shady maneuvering, very much like those games of chance that bordered on outright swindling. Antwerp was the site of a number of remarkable schemes until the city instituted strict controls. These included customers taking out policies in the Low Countries and Spain at the same time, man-made calamities, fictitious cargos supposedly shipwrecked, and so on. Even shadier, very often, were the life insurance plots in Antwerp —fraudulent schemes of which the insurers were the victims. J.A. Goris cites several macabre cases. Certain notaries in collusion with brokers would take out insurance on the life of a third party, naming themselves as beneficiaries. The latter, whom they declared to be in good health, was invariably gravely ill, or, if it appeared that he would not pass away within the brief time period stated in the policy (usually a few months), they would see to it that he was promptly dispatched.

In 1566, here is what happened to Paul van Hoboken, who was incurably ill. A notary named van Laer took out an insurance policy on his life, naming another notary, van Cothem, as beneficiary. The term was set at four months, during which time Hoboken "would be free to travel wherever he pleased, by land or by sea." It so happened that the deal also involved a wager on a fictitious voyage. If he died before the four months were up, van Cothem would receive the insured amount; the insurers had pledged not to ask him "for what reason or cause he has taken out insurance or assurance on the life of the aforesaid Paul," despite the legislative enactments expressly prohibiting this type of contract. Then van Laer advised Hoboken to place himself under the care of a very suspicious old Englishwoman. On the advice of his friends, Hoboken refused, but he did accept an invitation to dine at van Laer's home. Shortly thereafter, his widow attributed his death to "some poisonous and ruinous meat" that he had consumed during this meal. This episode, worthy of a horror story, was not an isolated incident. We are dealing here with a parasitic excrescence on a branch of business that, fortunately, as a rule was less picturesque. The important thing is that the development of insurance gave men a greater financial mastery over things and made them more independent of the world's vicissitudes by introducing an element of greater rationality into the workings of chance.

THE MERCHANT MENTALITY AND THE SCIENTIFIC SPIRIT

Perspectives had to be broadened. The increasing rationality of business organization involved a certain rationalization of thought and of life in general. This is not to say, of course, that the advance of science or what is usually called "free" thought proceeded automatically from the rise of the business bourgeoisie. Modern mechanistic science dates from Galileo and Descartes, not from the Renaissance, but although the great discoveries of the mind were the work of certain individuals, they required for their germination a fertile soil prepared by a propitious intellectual climate; improvement of the mind's tools and the development of attitudes and modes of behavior that encouraged the formulation of new questions and, in an implicit and tentative manner, suggested possible answers. Unfortunately, the history of knowledge sometimes neglects to examine the problems of collective conditioning—or, to be more precise, social conditioning. The mentality of an age is a vague abstraction; everything is a function of the social group.

Studies on Portuguese expansion reveal some significant transformations in this respect. In the texts recounting the voyages of discovery in the fifteenth century, everything concerned scientific problems—astronomical observations, the desire to settle the question of the shape of the earth, or the measuring of the arc of the meridian were added when revisions were made during the sixteenth century. Thus, since the first edition, a change in mentality had occurred. There are two manuscript editions of the *Chronicle of the Events in Guinea*; the first was written around 1460 by a courtier, the second in 1506. The latter contains far fewer moralizing digressions and learned quotations, but far more mathematical data. It is the work of a Moravian who had served as a notary for the German merchants in Lisbon and had himself engaged in both merchandising and printing.

We must not, however, confuse the mercantile spirit with the scientific spirit. What primarily interested the merchants was applied research, the utilitarian achievements of astronomers, cosmographers, and hydrographers. However limited their influence on the current practices of the seaman's trade may appear, the studies carried out in this domain yielded results of great intellectual value. In his *Esmeraldo de Situ Orbis* (1505), the Portuguese Duarte Pacheco, making only a few insignificant errors, stated the position of numerous latitudes; he also calculated to within five degrees the longitude of the meridian of Tordesillas, the dividing line between the Spanish and Portuguese empires in America; and, finally, he erred by only 4 percent in his estimation of the length of a meridian degree. This whole field of investigation witnessed considerable progress. Pedro Nunes, the author of a well known *Treatise on the Sphere* (1537), defined the nature of the loxodromic curve, and the

Fleming Mercator empirically discovered the projection technique which made possible decisive improvements in marine maps. All these discoveries were as yet merely scraps of knowledge—a few small building blocks to be used in the construction of a new cosmography that Copernicus had begun and Galileo would complete.

Like the treatises on bookkeeping, the treatises on nautical science, which increased in number and improved in quality during the sixteenth century, were part of the intellectual patrimony of the businessmen. One of the most widely used, though not the best, was the *Arte de Navegar* by the Spaniard, Pedro de Medina (1545), which was translated into several languages and adopted as a teaching manual. It also served as the inspiration for Michel Coignet's *New Course*, which was published in Antwerp in both Flemish and French and which the author dedicated to Agidius Hofman, a leading German merchant who specialized in African commerce and trade with the north and was a friend of Thomas Gresham and William of Orange. Coignet saluted him as a "true promoter of these so profitable and necessary inventions"; and, in fact, Hofman, well versed in the subject himself, had also patronized the work of Ortelius and the publication of his remarkable *Theatrum Orbis Terrarum*. Thus, the patronage of the businessmen was at first utilitarian in character. Their contributions—mainly financial, though occasionally intellectual—to the advancement of certain sciences were an integral part of their normal business activities and eventually benefited their own enterprises.

Their contributions to the progress of economic thought were a natural by-product of the evolution of business. During this period, it was the problems connected with money changing that caused the most ink to be spilled; the learned men approached these problems as jurists and theologians, though sometimes possessing a thorough knowledge of business practices, as in the case of Buoninsegni, a merchant turned Dominican, or the Belgian Jesuit, Lessius. The thinking of the big merchants bore the imprint of a pragmatism that rarely rose to the level of theory, whether in the manuals which described certain practices without offering any explanation of their mechanisms or in treatises on monetary and commercial policies. The reports by Gresham, for example, or those by the commissions in several occasions consulted by the English government, were not without their weaknesses: namely, a strong bias against Continental finance and an almost pathological belief in a foreign conspiracy against the pound sterling. So as to prove his own merits, Gresham no doubt exaggerated the importance of the clever maneuvers he executed on the Antwerp money market in order to maintain the price of the pound. However, these practitioners were able to observe certain fundamental relationships, among others, the one between the value of the currency and the fluctuations in the balance of payments. There were very few scholars in the sixteenth century—men like Copernicus, Mercado, or Jean Bodin—who were as deserving as they of the title of precursors of political economy.

To relate the merchant mentality to the intellectual history of the period, it is necessary to adopt a broader perspective, to take account of the more meaningful level of simple but essential phenomena. It was the merchant classes that gave to the world that spirit of exactitude which, as Lucien Febvre has clearly shown, most men of the sixteenth century lacked completely. Constantly working with weights and measures, and handling figures, they became more adept at thinking in quantitative terms; one obvious manifestation of this development was a more precise awareness of time. The birth dates of Erasmus, Rabelais, and Luther are not known, but Lucas Rem made a point of marking down in his diary the birth dates of every member of his family, as well as the dates of the outstanding events in the life of each of his twelve children—starting school, marriage, illnesses. In the same way, he kept an exact record of his business trips and of his own illnesses. Time was so valuable an element in certain operations that the merchant could not fail to acknowledge its tremendous importance.

Merchandising, bookkeeping, a more quantitative mentality, and, finally, the elaboration of a mathematical world view—there are large unquantitative mental zones from one end to the other of this chain, but it all holds together. Numbers were tools in the service of practical interests, before they became a means to greater understanding of science. In the long run, the rise of the merchant class was the most efficient agent in the transition (which proved to be a very slow process) from magical concepts to rational modes of thought, to the rationalzation of existence itself, one might say; but one must recognize that the force of circumstances imposed narrow limits on this development.

Was not the first, and most severely limiting factor the precariousness of human existence, in the biological sense of the term? Did the progress of knowledge that the merchant himself promoted, together with the increasing power of his moneyed wealth, assure the rich merchant of a better fate than that of his less fortunate contemporaries? At the present time, historical demography cannot furnish a statistical answer to this question. It is quite likely that even during this period, the "haves," thanks to their higher standard of living, had a longer life expectance than the "have-nots"; this hypothesis awaits statistical corroboration. However, in the family trees of many merchants, we can easily observe the fearful ravages of infant mortality, the frequent disappearance of young men, the paucity of individuals reaching what we today call old age.

The omnipresence of death constantly reminded man of the past— if he was ever tempted to forget it—of his weakness in a world that he had hardly begun to rationalize. "The guard who stands at the gates of the Louvre . . . ," Malherbe would write; nor did wealth offer much protection against death.

For information about epidemics, we turn again to Lucas Rem. When the plague struck Lisbon, people were dying all around him. He attributed his survival to the intervention of the Virgin Mary, St. Sebastian, and St. Roch. In his eyes, there was no more rational explanation, although Rem had taken the precaution of establishing his residence outside of the city, which he entered only when business required. To check the spread of the disease, more and more ports imposed quarantines. Arriving at Madeira from Lisbon in 1509, and standing on the boat to which he had been confined, Rem passed on to his factor, who was standing on the shore, the important orders that could not wait. All in all, the best defense that money afforded was the possibility of escape to a less exposed retreat; the wealthy, sometimes taking along their office equipment and their papers, withdrew to their country estates with the rest of their family. Moreover, they alone enjoyed the privilege of going "to take the waters" and of consulting the best doctors. But, in the sixteenth century, should we make much of that advantage? In the greatest families, like the Fuggers, the services of an astrologer were added to those of some medical luminary; the latter was not necessarily more effective than the former.

The situation can be roughly characterized thusly: the increasing mastery of the men of wealth represented the triumph of a certain kind of rationality, which also manifested itself at the cultural level; but for them as for the rest of mankind, the weight of the world was still overwhelming, as was the weight of an ancestral destiny, the force of tradition.

ACCESS TO CULTURE

What relationships existed among the growth of merchandising, the accumulations of money, and the development of this fertile century's most outstanding works?

One aspect of this problem concerns the accessibility of culture. This depended not only on how large a man's fortune was, but on when he had acquired it—we have already observed the contrast between the earlier and the later generations of the Fugger family. This banal observation relates specifically to one extremely important point. Latin, which was the indispensable language of scholars and which served both as a nutriment and an instrument of sixteenth-century humanism, was not normally a part of a merchant's education. Erasmus Schetz made a very thorough study of the classics in Cologne, a rather exceptional case in the early years of a dynasty. When he entered Cambridge, Thomas

Gresham was already the confirmed heir of a big business, as were Jacob Fugger's nephews or the sons whom Claus Stalburg placed under the tutelage of a student of the great Erasmus. To be able to send óne's sons to the university, and, in addition, to provide them with a first rate preceptor who often accompanied them and guided them from one faculty to another—this was a sign of great wealth. But we do not know to what extent such an education was characteristic of the merchant classes as a whole. Lucas Rem sent his son to Latin school without intending him for anything but business; the boy, however, upon acquiring noble status, would pursue an administrative career. Latin was not only the first step toward culture, it was also the first stage in a man's exodus from the business world, especially when the business was not out of the ordinary. Very frequently, learning this language was seen as a means of social advancement—from merchandising, for example, to law or to some career connected with the legal profession. The desire for culture remained a secondary consideration.

It would be wrong, however, to expect to find culture only among those who knew Latin, even in the sixteenth century. After all, Leonardo da Vinci had not attended school; he was a *uomo senze lettere*. Merchants—even those lacking a humanist education—were not insensitive to the beauties of nature and of art. They may not have expressed themselves too well on the subject, but, in effect, what Jacques Lesaige remembered of Venice is not very different from what Montaigne noted in his Journal, except that the merchant from Douai laid more stress on the city's manufacturing activities, which obviously fascinated him: "on a street where silk was being made in abundance . . . another where cotton was being refined . . . all workers making ordinance, and copper basins and products of iron." The Arsenal, Saint Mark's Square, and Venetian women made the same impression on both travelers. In 1509, Lucas Rem sojourned in Rome at his own expense on a ten day vacation. Accompanied by one of the Welsers, a curial prelate, he visited all the sights: "the Pope's white palace, all the treasures of the churches, the old buildings and the new"; he regretted having so little time at his disposal. Was he merely a curious tourist? Such curiosity is not an insignificant factor in the history of civilization. By virtue of their endless traveling, the merchants, consciously or unconsciously, played a major role in the dissemination of cultural goods of all sorts: from the most banal fashions and customs (while in Venice, Lesaige discovered the fork and the fan) to more sublime artistic pleasures. The most popular of the arts provides some examples of this.

For those who could not afford to surround themselves with truly artistic adornments, music was the most accessible source of esthetic pleasure. A musical instrument (some kind of flute, perhaps) like that of little Balthazer Paumgartner, seems to have been a fixture in many bourgeois homes. At the house of the burgomaster of Reval, where he had gone to make some sort of payment, Tonnis Smidt noticed a harpsichord—a sign of unusual wealth. Choral singing was even more common than instrumental music since it was a less expensive form of entertainment and was closely bound up with the practice of religion. Although confraternities may have diminished in importance, the church was still the most popular gathering place, especially for a colony of merchants in a foreign country. It was the hub of company life and a center of musical activity.

A systematic study of a number of posthumous inventories would be necessary in order to confirm these observations on the importance of music. Such a study would also throw light on the question of the merchant's reading habits. Disregarding the libraries of the illustrious financiers who by their very wealth must be classified as exceptions, we are reduced to a few scattered pieces of information. We know Paul Meyer owned practically no books at all. Claus Stalburg, on the other hand, owned about thirty volumes, mostly religious works, including two confessors' *summas*, a few chronicles, and translations of Caesar, Virgil, and Terence. Stalburg, then, did not know Latin (or did not know it well enough) and so he also had to read Pierre de Crescent, the classic writer on medieval agronomy, in German translation. All this was reading matter for a man of varied interests (Melanchthon called himself the friend of such a man); humanism would be his sons' interest. In the Ruiz family, Simon's nephew, who made a career in the Church, was the first to possess a library worthy of a cultured man (although Spain had been importing large quantities of books from Lyons). The collections owned by the business magnates, or more often by their descendants, were of a different order entirely. In the Fugger family, it was Ulrich, Jakob's brother, who first put together the nucleus of a library in 1509; it was by way of an endowment for the benefit of the Dominicans of Augsburg and was a mere trifle compared to what later generations would amass, not only books, but Greek and Latin manuscripts, coins and medallions, engravings, paintings, and sculptures. At the behest of Anton and especially Raymund, Hans Dernschwam, chief of the Fugger foreign trading offices in Hungary for twenty years, went around the country collecting Latin inscriptions. Preserved in the Fugger archives is the manuscript of a day-book that Dernschwam kept during a trip to Constantinople and Asia Minor (1553–1555); it is an extremely interesting text which reads like a commercial agent's report but, at the same time, attests to the author's profound knowledge of archeology and epigraphy. It was to this same Dernschwam that Sebastian Munster dedicated his *Rudimenta Mathematica* in 1551. Both the Schetzes and Gian Carlo Affaitadi owned priceless collections of books and antiques that were famous in their time.

The big bankers devoted a great deal of time and money to the museums that they set up both in their urban residences and in their castles—sometimes to the detriment of their business activities, unless they simply gave up business altogether. Hans Jakob Fugger, a humanist who found finance utterly bewildering, was the company's director from 1560 on and did not fare very well in business. But he knew Latin, Greek, Hebrew, Italian, French, Hungarian, Czech, and Polish, was an accomplished philologist, numismatist, and musician, and was especially interested in iconography, genealogy, and history. His brother Ulrich spent so much money on cultural items that the family was driven to obtain an interdict limiting his expenses. While the treasures accumulated by the wealthy flattered their penchant for ostentation (and also constituted an investment of a sort), these men were not merely satisfying their own vanity. For quite a few of them, such lavishness was the manifestation of highly refined taste, coupled with extensive knowledge—in short, of a veritable passion for humanism. Of course, all this could not but benefit the intellectuals of this age.

PATRONS OF THE ARTS

Naturally, the personal works of humanist merchants had less influence on the progress of scholarship and the flowering of the arts than their patronage. One of the principal aspects of this activity, often on a modest level, was the providing of scholarships, which were merely a special form of religious or charitable endowment. Also important, and more of an innovation, was the subsidization of publishing enterprises. In 1530, Johann Selhorst, an average merchant of Reval, financed the publication of the first printed Estonian book (in this particular case, religious zeal was the motivating factor). In other instances, the motives were less traditional. For a period of ten years, Ulrich Fugger gave Henri Estienne a regular stipend (along with various gifts), thus enabling the latter to maintain his own printing shop in Geneva; and the publications of this great Hellenist always contained some acknowledgement of his gratitude. Great merchants, as well as princes, offered scholars secure livelihoods as their secretaries or librarians—positions that gave them access to their patrons' precious collections. Nor was the munificence of the wealthy denied those men who, like Erasmus, were secure enough not to have to depend too much on the generosity of their friends. For patronage created a relationship that was hardly in keeping with today's widespread belief in the dignity of the intellectual.

The dithyrambs accompanying expressions of thanks cannot but strike one as rather platitudinous. Without establishing a hard and fast distinction (which would be artificial) between scholars and men of letters, it would seem that the latter were the masters of self-seeking flattery. And I am not referring here merely to those Apollos of the *collège* so skillfully portrayed by Lucien Febvre. One need only think of Aretino serving up the same compliment to both the Fuggers and Gian Carlo Affaitadi: he called them more generous than a king. Under these conditions, certain beneficiaries received from their patron less esteem than gratuities. Their servile demeanor rather suggests the mentality of a domestic. However, patronage cannot be reduced to this degrading dialectic. In the sixteenth century, the artist's condition improved both morally and materially, although, by present standards, the monetary values placed on his works and on his talent were still rather low. In 1520, while in Antwerp, Albrecht Dürer drew a large number of portraits which he generally presented to his models for *one* florin apiece. Though unhappy with the financial balance sheet for his trip, did Dürer consider himself underpaid? And this question leads to other questions. There is nothing in his diary that suggests he was ever treated with anything less than the greatest deference. On the evening of his arrival, the Fuggers' factor offered him a sumptuous repast, and the Portuguese and Italian merchants with whom he visited, as well as the Germans, welcomed him as a guest who did honor to their homes.

Almost every branch of art in the sixteenth century can be shown to have had its connections with the business world, even if one simply classifies the commissions, and enumerates the works executed for merchants. The Fuggers' house in Rome, of which nothing remains, was decorated by a student of Raphael. In 1508, Giorgione and Titian worked on the frescos at the Fondaco dei Tedeschi, where the latter was appointed as a broker in 1516. Just as the Church provided prebends, so commerce offered sinecures, the income from which supplemented the artists' proceeds from numerous sales to a business clientele. The increased contacts between this clientele and the artists resulted in a marked commercialization of art.

Since the Middle Ages, it is true, works of art represented for the Italian merchants merely one type of commodity among others. In the sixteenth century, the market for these particular commodities ex-

panded appreciably, especially for those artistic products that had benefited from technological progress: books more than anything, naturally,
but also engravings, the reproduction and publication of which developed alongside the printing of texts. This observation applies even more
to the decorative arts (like the prosperous tapestry workshops in the Low
Countries) and all the so-called minor arts. The business spirit thus
spread into new areas, sometimes to the detriment of the quality of the
workmanship. No sooner had the octavos (this format was itself a commercial innovation) of Aldus Manutius appeared—real philological and
typographical masterpieces—than someone in Lyons began turning out
skillful counterfeits, bearing no indication of the date or place of publication. The quality of the paper and of the type in these facsimiles was
not poor, though they did contain errata. Since they were less expensive,
they sold faster than the originals of the great Venetian humanist.
Literary piracy was born. The leading printers had to possess, not only
technical skill and literary taste, but good commercial sense—qualities
that were not lacking in such men as Sébastien Gryphe of Lyons or
Christophe Plantin of Antwerp. The double-entry account books of the
latter are among the finest that have been preserved from this period.
Certain artists accommodated themselves to these new conditions,
Dürer more than any other, who published his own engravings. One of
his reasons for journeying to the Low Countries was, as he put it, to "sell
some art." And he carefully recorded all transactions: "I sold 2 Adam
and Eves, one marine monster, one Jerome, one knight, one Nemesis,
one Eustace, one complete folio, plus 17 engravings, 8 quarter-folios, 19
other engravings on wood and 7 bad engravings on wood, 2 books and
10 small Passions on wood, for a total of 8 florins."

Did sixteenth-century art give expression to ideas and feelings peculiar
to the business world? The clients from this milieu favored certain
genres, such as portrait painting; moreover, their activities were, for
certain artists, a great source of inspiration. For example, Dürer's taste
for the exotic, his curiosity about the strange objects brought back from
overseas (one expression of his passionate pursuit of the unknown) ac-

corded perfectly with the businessman's fascination with discovery, which drove adventurous men toward ever more distant horizons in pursuit of ever greater profits. At first glance, the most common themes in Renaissance art, particularly the mythological material that was so frequently employed, do not seem to lend themselves to such an interpretation since it is so much simpler to see all this as merely a return to antiquity; but is the subject matter the essence of a work of art? The analyses of Pierre Francastel, who perceives a new vision in Italian painting of the Quattrocento—the discovery and representation of space conquered and rationalized—provide some brilliant insights into the profound relationships between the evolution of art and that of a society in which the rationalizing power of money was asserting itself. Italy led the way from the fifteenth century on.

In its efforts to substantiate these insights with more specific details, the sociology of art has encountered obstacles that it has not yet surmounted and that are, in fact, insurmountable when each work of art is considered in isolation; what it contains and what it expresses cannot be easily elucidated. Difficulties are also encountered in trying to perceive not only the characteristics but also the depth and the limits of the change of mentality within a social milieu which was in a constant state of flux and whose boundaries were indeterminate. If the realistic character of portrait painting can be imputed to the tastes of the merchants, who merely wanted a likeness of themselves fixed on canvas, one must also recognize that these tastes infected other strata of society.

One must resist the tendency to reduce all Renaissance culture to what went on in the courts of princes or in coteries of scholars, without any regard to the social context. For the dissemination of this culture outside of Italy, the expansion of Italian commerce was absolutely essential. But the imitation or adoption of foreign influences was only one more or less important aspect shared by the diverse civilizations coexisting on the European continent. It is by considering the loci at which these influences first took root and the level at which they were thoroughly assimilated that one must evaluate the contribution of the men of wealth to the development of culture in the sixteenth century. As far as the breadth and the originality of their contributions are concerned, one must be very cautious in one's judgments—the intention being not to minimize the dependency of the cultural element vis-à-vis the social element (the limits of this relationship were defined of course by the creativity of the thinkers and artists), but rather to give full weight to the complexity of social life, whose advance was much too slow and too ambiguous to overturn the structures of the mind.

the sons would go on business trips for their father or another merchant; during these years of apprenticeship, when there was no chance for advancement in their father's service, they sometimes discovered the path to success in a foreign city—or, at least, achieved independence.

Among more prosperous families, things went differently: there was room and work for everyone, under the father's leadership, especially in a large family enterprise where the sons were given an increasingly important role. So it was with the Imhofs of Nuremberg. When Hans the Elder died in 1499, his five sons were already active in the company; Hans the younger, whose share of the capital amounted to 100 florins in 1481, had increased his share to 17,650 florins by the time of his death in 1522. His son, Andreas, in his turn, started out with 20 florins in 1508 and by 1522, was worth 3,630 florins. Thus, generally speaking, the large enterprise made for a more closely knit family, from which were excluded those members who preferred (and could afford) to live off their private incomes—and, of course, the black sheep, a notorious example of which we find in the Paumgartner family. Anton, one of the sons of Hans Paumgartner the younger, was a ne'er-do-well who married a rich heiress in 1540 and treated her so badly that after three years they legally separated; whereupon his father barred him from the business and stripped him of any claim to the landed property of the family.

In a social milieu where family and career were so closely joined, marriages were arranged in the manner of a business transaction. Contracts fixing the size of the wife's dowry or a widow's dower were elaborate, carefully worded documents. Even if the parties had few possessions, a great deal of ink was spilled, a veritable boon for the lawyers of the day. Among people who were more well-to-do, the wedding ceremony was a particularly extravagant affair which produced an abundance of gifts. One can picture Lucas Rem computing the total value of the gifts he received on his wedding day: all of Augsburg's most illustrious citizens were on his guest list. Jakob Fugger and the bishop each presented him with a roebuck. And every single item was appraised, even the religious figure (worth 1 florin) sent by the prioress of Saint

Catherine (a Welser). Even more important was the fact that the great dynasties of the business world, like their royal counterparts, adhered to a definite matrimonial policy. The leader of the Affaitadi, at the beginning of the sixteenth century, was Gian Francesco of Lisbon, who died in 1528. He was succeeded by his nephew, Gian Carlo of Antwerp, who married his predecessor's daughter, Lucretia; the latter, widowed in 1555, then married Balthazer Schetz. The Fuggers' partnership with the Thurzos was strengthened by two marriages, celebrated under the sign of the copper trade: one between Jakob Fugger's nephew and Hans Thurzo's daughter, the other between the former's niece and the latter's son.

The principal merchant families of every city were linked together by a multitude of interlocking alliances. Any study of their business operations inevitably entails genealogical research. Despite, or perhaps because of its extraordinary cohesion, this aristocracy of trade was subject to fierce internecine struggles.

In his memoirs, Heinrich Brokes, who was burgomaster of Lübeck at the beginning of the seventeenth century, vaunts the illustriousness of his maternal ancestors; his father, who had achieved success by dint of hard work, had in 1552 married a young girl who, though poor, was descended from the most illustrious families. On the other hand, Heinrich deplored his brother Hans's marriage in 1586; the bride was pretty, but coquettish and given to idleness and, besides, was descended on her mother's side from an old but not very respectable family. The author's personal opinions are his responsibility, but we may note in passing that pecuniary considerations did not preclude the merchant family's worrying about such things as respectability and morality. It is more interesting, but more difficult, to find any expressions of feeling, for these people were very sparing of their confidences.

Because such documents are so rare, the letters that Balthazar Paumgartner and Magdalena Behaim (whom he married in 1583) exchanged during the years 1582–1598 are priceless indeed. He often went to Lucca on business, while she stayed in Augsburg; after ten years of marriage, they still wrote each other regularly every week. While they were still fiancés, their rhetoric sometimes lacked levity, as witness this New Year's greeting (December 22, 1582): "God's grace, His blessing, and His mercy, together with the complete well-being—eternal and temporal—of thy soul and body: this is what I wish thee, honorable and virtuous, kind and faithful fiancée so dear to my heart, for a blissful new year rich in kindnesses and joy. May the good Lord grant this to us all through Jesus Christ, the newborn child, our only Savior and Redeemer. Amen."

But in recalling their farewell, he expresses his affection in more direct terms. Balthazar cannot dispel this image from his memory: "and since then, few hours, very few hours, have passed that I have not thought of thee. . . . Last Friday, all night long, I dreamt of thee, I hope that this signifies nothing but good." Later on, when more space was devoted to headaches and stomach aches and everyday occurrences—such as the baptism of a compatriot's twenty-eighth child—Magdalena, having received no mail for quite some time, complained about this in language that was both simple and natural: "Three weeks now without hearing from thee and, possibly, no mail between now and next Saturday— which would make me very unhappy. And I cannot help thinking of the old proverb: Out of sight, out of mind." But she knew from the business letters he was sending his brother that her husband was very busy.

In another of Magdalena's letters, the image of her son appears. The child wants his absent father to know that he has learned to play a dance on his musical instrument. When dealing with children, was the businessman's hardness tempered by a modicum of gentleness? Indeed, for adolescents who often started working at the age of 12, even in a comfortable milieu, life must have been hard. Yet his child's suffering tore from Lucas Rem a moment of emotion (a rarity in his diary); after weeks of suffering, his eight-month-old son passed away: "in my life I have never seen a more piteous spectacle." Even illegitimate children were the objects of a solicitude which could almost be called humane. Preparing a register of his offspring, Rem first listed the five children he had fathered before his marriage, all by the same woman, when he lived in Antwerp. He had them taken away from their mother in order to secure them a respectable station in life. One of his bastard daughters, after finishing her schooling, took a job with him; he later remarked that she had "earned almost all" the money spent on her—generosity carried its own obligations. A son, on the other hand, caused him nothing but disappointment. Rem found jobs for him in Frankfurt, Ulm, Venice, Tarvisio, again in Germany, then Antwerp; wherever he was, he behaved badly or ran away: "This is why I cross myself and commend him to God." We would certainly need many more written confidences of this sort if we wished to go beyond mere anecdote and depict the sensibilities of an entire class, but at least we can catch a glimpse of how much their sensibilities differed from ours in certain respects.

A woman's role in merchant society was not limited to conjugal duties. As in every other class in Catholic countries, young girls were urged, sometimes even forced, to enter a convent. This was a social and even a demographic problem. The chronicles relate how, in 1561, a young niece of Anton Fugger escaped from the convent of Saint Catherine, where her mother and a Jesuit had placed her against her will, and eventually got married, under the protection of a Protestant relative. But there is another aspect of the feminine condition that merits more consideration—the important role that women often played in the business world.

There was Madeleine Lartissat of Avignon, for example (although hers was a rather extraordinary career). The adulterine daughter of a Medici, she equipped ships in Marseilles and engaged in trading under her own name. She was also, J. Billioud informs us, "commercial directress in charge of weapons and prizes" for the general of the galleys, who helped her forget her unhappy marriage. Among the larger merchants, the wife's influence often extended beyond household affairs; Jakob Fugger's nephews were openly hostile toward his wife, whom they suspected of excessive zeal in the interest of her own clan. There were also countless widows who, in spite of the law, managed to rid themselves of their guardians and executors and ran their businesses by themselves. The widow of Wilhelm Bresser of Lübeck, whom we met earlier, proceeded in just this fashion. She became a widow for the second time in 1574, twenty-one years after her first husband's death; the result was an endless succession of lawsuits between the children of the two marriages. In the course of these proceedings, she repeatedly denied knowing how to read or write, but the business letters (a few of which have been preserved) were addressed to her.

These brief glimpses notwithstanding, the reality of the merchant's wife, even more than that of her husband, remains hidden behind a curtain of conventional rhetoric which paints an image of the virtuous matron alongside that of the honorable merchant. The well-to-do were confident of their dignity but did not stand on ceremony; they displayed their wealth with pride—in their homes, their luxurious attire, their jewelry. Posthumous inventories of their possessions have provided us with detailed information concerning all these items, but more systematic studies will have to be made before we can determine the subtle gradations of opulence. In general, furniture was rather crude, except in the homes of the very rich. On the other hand, everywhere were found an impressive number of metal utensils which, though functional, were sometimes skillfully wrought out of silver, copper, or pewter. One good indication of the size of a family's fortune was the quantity of the noblest metal in its possession. The emphasis was on visible, tangible wealth, the enjoyment of which was not without esthetic considerations; but which, in case of need, could always be converted into cash.

In a century of drinkers and heavy eaters, the most ordinary merchant had a supply of goblets. At the end of the narration of his pilgrimage to Jerusalem, published at his own expense in 1518, a silk trader from Douai by the name of Jacques Lesaige described himself in these terms: "He has drawn the corks of many bottles and flasks, I pray that God will pardon him. Amen."

Whether they were well-to-do merchants who inevitably had a suburban residence (sometimes just outside the walls of the city) in the midst of a garden, vineyard, or hop-field or big businessmen living in princely luxury, these men of the sixteenth century were never abstemious misers. Certain displays of prodigality reveal the characteristics of the nouveau riche—if indeed it is true that the son and son-in-law of Ambroise Höchstetter squandered nearly 10,000 florins on one night of feasting—if, that is, the chroniclers were not merely exercising their imaginations. In any case, from roaming the world in search of profit, the most sober individuals discovered new ways to spend money which soon became fasionable everywhere. In Lisbon, Lucas Rem purchased cats, parrots, and "other pleasing curiosities"; in Antwerp, paintings and objets d'art. Culture was one form of pleasure.

THE TEMPORAL AND THE SPIRITUAL

The humanist merchants, infatuated with their recently acquired or prospective nobility and obsessed with their genealogy, were to a great extent living in the past. Their contributions, in their capacity as businessmen, to sixteenth-century humanism—a greater sense of exactitude, the extension of empirical knowledge—were not sufficient to alter the basic orientation of a way of thinking that was unable to shake off certain powerful influences: first, the cult of antiquity, which superstitious men invented with great delight; second, the conception of a "universe peopled with demons," which had not yet been replaced by the coherent universe of the mathematicians; and finally, traditional religious beliefs, which were so strong that one hesitates to speak of a secularization of culture (although such things as the widening gap between the Christian ideal and political realities or the humanization of art, particularly in its sources of inspiration, do indeed point in this direction). During the sixteenth century, religion often served as a mediator between wealth and art, but one could hardly regard this as its sole function. It still stood at the center of cultural life, at the center of life itself.

In this century "which wanted to believe," humanity could not but submit to the domination of an omnipresent religion, which dictated how each individual was to order his life and affected his way of viewing the world. This inescapable fact produced certain developments in the business world, which had less to do with the specific forms of devotion among the merchants than with the obstacles to mercantile activity inherent in the Church's traditional teachings concerning usury. The problem cannot be reduced to the temporal relationships between the merchant, on the one hand, and the Church and its members on the other; for it was always posed in terms of the individual conscience. In any event, the churches were part of society and had to be reckoned with.

For two centuries or more, the Roman Church had been assisted by bankers in collecting the revenues that the papal state required. Certain churchmen had no qualms about associating with merchants as partners rather than as clients. Such relationships lead to an equally realistic observation: the merchant considered the Church hierarchy from top to bottom a power whose good will must be won and preserved. There was no better way to accomplish this than by having one's own sources of information within that structure. Every merchant family included a certain number of ecclesiastics, whose position corresponded to the family's importance locally or internationally. This meant that the most eminent families always had a son, nephew, uncle, or cousin serving as a prelate in Rome itself. The same Christopher Welser who guided Lucas Rem through the splendors of the Eternal City was an apostolic protonotary and secret chamberlain to the Pope, however, he was not directly involved with the Welsers' foreign trading office. On the other hand, Bernhard Zink, the Fuggers' representative in Rome from 1501 on, used his position to accumulate a number of ecclesiastical honors and prebends throughout Europe. At the same time, Hans Thurzo, bishop of Breslau (the family also had a bishop in Olmutz), was rendering the Fuggers important services. It would be interesting, from the viewpoint of Church history, social history, and the history of ideas, to know just what proportion of abbey and chapter members were merchants' sons. Neither the frequency nor the importance of these relationships was in any way diminished by the rupture of Christian unity. Because of the barriers that this event created, the merchants—no matter which camp they had joined, either by personal choice or in deference to the expressed sympathies of their community as a whole—had to proceed even more cautiously vis-à-vis the ecclesiastical authorities. The guardians of orthodoxy were becoming ever more distrustful and kept a particularly close watch on those who traveled or had business relations abroad. If one did not think correctly, one's business would suffer: this would explain the certificate of Catholicity delivered in 1577 by the curé of a Rouen parish to a native merchant who was apparently having problems with the Spanish Inquisition.

If need be, however, these barriers could be raised. Most of the merchants who were driven out of Antwerp or voluntarily left the city for religious reasons, continued to maintain a correspondent or even a branch office there. Philip II went on dealing with the Hanseatic merchants, avowed heretics, while the Pope, in order to facilitate matters for his grain suppliers in Danzig, was able to dampen the passions of the "counter-reformers" in the area. Despite this widespread opportunism, men remained as attached to their beliefs as ever.

God's name appeared in all commercial documents. Every letter of exchange, without exception, began with the words, *Laus Deo;* charter parties never mentioned a ship without adding, "may God protect it"; one could give an endless number of examples. These were by no means merely concessions to custom, set phrases prescribed by polite usage. Charitable provisions in wills, philanthropy, and pious donations are tangible evidence of the universality of faith. Business success, familial well-being, escaping a shipwreck or a plague unscathed—such good fortune was always attributed to the intervention of God and His Son, His Holy Mother and His saints. It goes without saying that the fear of Hell was a very important element in this faith.

At one point in Lucas Rem's diary, "Jesus Maria" is suddenly replaced by a simple "Jesus." This foreshortening is not accompanied by any commentary, since our merchant was no theologian, but the slight shift raises the problem of the businessman's attitude toward the Reformation. This shift is not insignificant, for, although this diary does not reflect the controversies or the tumultuous incidents that accompanied the Reformation in Augsburg, it does throw considerable light on the religious psychology of the period.

During the first ten years of the century, this Protestant-to-be appeared as a devout believer in the Holy Virgin and all the saints. When his ship dropped anchor at Coruña in 1508, he undertook a two day journey to Santiago de Compostella with the ship's captain, and, the following year, stopping again at Coruña, he found, much to his regret, that he could not repeat his pilgrimage, lest a favorable wind come up during his absence. In that same year, 1509, he traveled to Italy and Provence, following the pilgrim's itinerary: Loreto, Saint Maximin, Sainte-Baume, and a detour from Arles to Saintes-Maries de la Mer, then on to Marseilles, Aix, and Tarascon. At every shrine, he conscientiously examined all the relics. In 1510, he stopped at the shrine of Our Lady of Guadalupe, confessed his sins, and went into ecstasies upon hearing of the miracles that regularly took place there. Shortly thereafter, he went to admire Montserrat. These were all traditional acts of piety. Jacques Lesaige of Douai was also following tradition when he had the coat of arms of the patriarchate of Jerusalem painted on his sign board, together with the motto: "Praised be God. I have returned from there."

Pilgrimages, relics, cults devoted to the saints—all the old practices, ridiculed by Erasmus and his followers, still dominated the religious life of the merchants. The question of whether or not humanism opened the way, at least for the most cultured individuals, to a more personal religion (the very religion that the Erasmians professed) has not been very thoroughly explored. At Augsburg, while a false mysticism of very dubious origins was gaining favor with the aristocracy of finance (even Anton Welser was somewhat taken by it), Jakob Fugger was still requesting indulgences for his own sins. Indeed, it would be paradoxical to expect from laymen the definitions of dogma that the meditations of clerics were confusedly elaborating. Over and above all the divisions, the reformers, without exception, accused the established Church of lack of faith and demanded a new faith—or, at least, profound changes in the old one. Was the world of business, because of its own peculiar anxieties, predisposed to welcome the reformers' message? Unfortunately, very few historians of the Reformation have bothered to study the religious sensibilities of the faithful as a major contributing factor to change; this is all the more reason for our lack of information classified according to social class.

REFORMATION AND CAPITALISM

The problem of the merchant class's receptiveness to Protestant preachings has been attacked from another angle. Lutheranism quickly established itself in the cities of Germany, and the merchants had much to do with carrying it to the Low Countries. Twenty years later, in these same Low Countries, as in Great Britain, Calvinism would find an excellent breeding ground. Historians have been tempted to seek in the Reformation the religious expression of a social movement, but the temptation has rarely produced any serious attempts at research along these lines. Can we speak of a revolt aiming at both the traditional religious order and the traditional social order? A cursory survey of the period might well lead to this conclusion, but once the researcher begins to probe for specific data, he encounters so many difficulties that most historians of the Reformation prefer not to bother with the question at all.

Let us review those facts that may be considered incontrovertible. The Reformation did not gain the adherence of all sectors of the merchant bourgeoisie. Even in those regions where it established its predominance, it was the lower classes, that is, the petit bourgeois artisans, who assured its victory over the conservatism of the rich merchants. Lübeck offers a striking example of this process. Nothing seems more natural at first glance. Jakob Fugger declared himself "utterly opposed to Lutheranism"; was it not clear from Luther's thundering against usury that he wanted to see the Fuggers and all their kind removed from power? In his views on money and society, Luther was as traditional as one could be. Luther, yes—but what of Lutheranism? A much more difficult question to answer. In any case, some merchants, including a few from the leading ranks, adopted the Lutheran confession. Under popular pressure, Augsburg opted for the Reformation despite the opposition of the powerful financiers. (Certain members of the business aristocracy, however—even some of the Fuggers—also embraced the heresy.) In sum, and there is no doubt of this, the merchant classes did not side *en bloc* with Rome or with the Reformation. This was no more the case before than after the second great wave—the one led by Calvin—to which some have sought to attribute special significance in this regard.

Calvinism did contain a doctrinal innovation in that it formally sanctioned interest on loans. To minds more adept at exegesis and at juggling abstract ideas than at historical observation and social analysis, this was the source of the capitalist spirit (or, at least, its legitimation) and hence, a powerful stimulus to the development of capitalism. Without being heeded, historians have also noted that the Catholic businessmen of the sixteenth century displayed no less dynamism than their Calvinist competitors, even after the balance of economic power finally shifted to the northwestern part of Europe, which was mainly Protestant. It seems, moreover, that long before Calvin, Italian businessmen already possessed the economic virtues of the Puritans. In a treatise published in Venice in 1573 and translated into French in 1582, but originally written in the fifteenth century, the Ragusan merchant, Benedetto Cotrugli, wrote: "the work of the merchants is ordained for the sake of mankind's salvation." Can one conceive of a more metaphysical paean to the entrepreneurial spirit? The notion of a close connection between profits and grace, the clear conscience of the men who were growing rich, the conviction that success, far from displeasing God, was, on the contrary, proof of his favor—all these things were as common among

Catholics as Protestants. Jakob Fugger's "rich by the grace of God" was echoed by this inscription adorning the Bourse of Valencia: *Mercator sic agens divitiis redundabit et tandem vita fruetur aeterna.*

Perhaps Puritan morality reinforced certain traits, particularly that hardness toward oneself and toward others that manifested itself economically as the spirit of investment. But to test the validity of this hypothesis, it would still be necessary to examine the actual economic behavior of businessmen and not merely the precepts contained in the manuals on morality. If the extent to which the Calvinist ideology acted as an economic stimulant has been greatly overestimated, this is partly due to a lack of knowledge concerning the character of the economic developments in both the Catholic and the Lutheran countries; but it is mainly because of the undue significance attached to the Calvinist santion of interest.

CONSCIENCE AND INTEREST

The effects of the Church's obstinate defense of its doctrine on this matter (*pecunia pecuniam non parit*) were both far-reaching and limited. In practice, in order to make his capital bear fruit without his incurring the infamous accusation of usury, the merchant had a considerable number of means at his disposal—though not quite the sixty-three techniques for making money devised by Rabelais Panurge. Certain facets of the enormous but disjointed edifice erected by the doctors were so formalistic that one is very often justified in asking whether the authors were the dupes of their own super-subtle naiveté or whether they were simply terribly clever at concealing their inevitable acquiescence to current practices behind a wall of rigorous principles. In any case, the upward surge of profits was not noticeably affected. But this is not to imply that the Catholic merchant had been freed from all scruples regarding the legitimacy of his operations.

On the other hand, the interdicts issued by the Church had a tremendous impact on men's consciences. In particularly thorny matters beyond the ken of their confessors, even the boldest of businessmen would frequently consult the most eminent theologians. Thus, in 1532, some Spaniards from Antwerp solicited the opinion of the Sorbonne on certain exchange contracts. If the response was negative, there were always various ways of circumventing the restrictions. When in 1571 Pius V formally interdicted the deposit or fair-to-fair exchange, the Bonvisi of Lyons wrote: "it was with great difficulty that we have served our friends, and it was necessary to practice a measure of deception." In the judgment of Simon Ruiz, who, as a matter of conscience, refused to take interest in this manner, the Bonvisi were audacious indeed.

Flexibility on the part of theologians was augmented by extensive, nuanced interpretations by the businessmen. Together, these two factors resulted in practices that were a far cry from what a literal mind might deduce from principles. It is certain, in any case, that every type of transaction that had been condemned rapidly reappeared in a different form, with its basic mechanism unchanged. It is hardly surprising that the Italians displayed the greatest versatility in this game; but they did not feel any less like good Christians because of it.

The whole matter will be clarified if we consider how they defined "scruples" in this century. What counted was absolute observance of the rules. In 1577, a factor of the Fuggers in Spain wrote, apropos of the Genoese, Lazar Doria, that he had had "so sensitive a conscience that he never engaged in any of those exchanges or trade practices which the preachers and theologians here denounce in their writings and orations." In his will, this same Doria declared that he had no need to make restitution (it was an old medieval practice to make restitution as one's final penance), because the capital he had invested, in operations that were probably not very Catholic, did not belong to him. Cynicism and hypocrisy? To assert this would be to define morality in terms of our own logic, which is not quite the same as that of the sixteenth century. However, one is tempted to believe that Matthäus Schwarz, Jakob Fugger's chief bookkeeper, penned the following note in a moment of sincerity: "*Nota bene famulus. Interesse ist höflich gewuchert. Finanzen ist hoflich gestolen* "; (interest is a polite word for usury; finance, a polite word for theft). The term *interest* was commonly employed in texts to designate something licit, such as *lucrum cessans* or some other invention of the theologians. There were probably some merchants who perceived the discrepancy between the letter and the spirit, but why should this stop them if the doctors were ready to declare that the proper form was being observed?

Putting his finger on the weakness of traditional doctrine concerning usury, Calvin, with irresistible logic, clarified the issue for the benefit of those who shared his faith—an issue that the Church had obstinately regarded as the crux of its economic morality, which was by now completely obsolete, as if it could not see that the real problems posed by money revolved around the question of profits, not interest. Camouflaging interest was a purely technical matter; the important thing was that the upsurge in profits, with the concomitant glorification of the entrepreneurial spirit, and the consolidation of capitalist structures in the sixteenth-century economy were causing every church considerable difficulties. Every faith had its strict and loose interpreters. The bankers, said Erasmus, "*quorum artem video probe defendi posse. . . .*" Was there some connection between openmindedness on this subject and the least traditional of faiths? The Roman Church had more need of subtle distinctions but the most advanced Protestants felt compelled to appeal to equity and charity, a form of *lucrum moderatum* and no less flexible.

Although confusion reigned in the realm of ideas—Jesuit casuistry had developed alongside of Puritan morality—it was everywhere giving way to a tendency that, in the long run, was favorable to the spirit of the century, in other words, to the comprehension of reality. In the final analysis, it was this very confusion that reflected most accurately the spirit of the century and the mentality of the merchant. Nothing except material obstacles could halt the expansion of his enterprises. At the same time, he felt a need to be reassured about the consequences in his after-life of activities that he sometimes felt were not in harmony with the religious philosophy that he and his fellow men still accepted. He wanted to believe that his two paramount goals in life—power and wealth on this earth and the salvation of his soul—were not irreconcilable; and, provided he did not overstep certain limits, the theologians did not deny him this double satisfaction. This compact, the bases for which had existed since the Middle Ages, excluded the possibility of a revolt by the moneyed interests against the faith. The businessman had no worthwhile alternative to Heaven, where he was sure a place had been reserved for him, nor did he have any fundamental objections to the existing social order.

XI

The Merchant and the Established Order

The rapid growth of commerce during the Middle Ages introduced a foreign body into feudal society—the bourgeoisie. But not every bourgeoisie was a mercantile one (and this qualification remained valid for the sixteenth century as well). The social changes resulting from the expansion of trade at the beginning of the modern era can hardly be summed up in a simple formula like "the rise of the bourgeoisie"—a phrase full of overtones for today's reader which tend to distort the human realities of the sixteenth century.

Not only in the realm of ideas, but in the very language of the period, the word *bourgeoisie* assumed a strictly urban connotation. One was a bourgeois (burgess) of a certain town, a *civis*; and, in principle, this flattering title, in keeping with its original definition, still restricted the bourgeois to his city, setting him apart, not only from the inhabitants of the countryside, but even from the majority of his fellow townsmen, who were simply the inhabitants of their town, not bourgeois. These juridical delimitations, this hierarchy of orders, should not be considered an adequate representation of social reality, but it is important to recognize that the existence of these divisions shaped the relationships among social groups and indicated real structural differences between this society and that of the nineteenth century (the model from which our terminology is derived). In a city, the principal line of social cleavage ran between an oli-

garchy and the majority of the population, which included certain bourgeois as well as the ordinary inhabitants—that is, in terms of classes,
petty bourgeois and genuine proletarians. The merchants represented a
fraction, often the largest component, of the minority, which dominated
the town politically by virtue of its economic strength and which used
this political power to further its own interests. The most complete
expression of this identification of political power and mercantile interests was the merchant republic, the free city, which in Italy and Germany during the Middle Ages, achieved total independence. The
leading businessmen were the masters, the glittering ornaments, the
glory of these cities. Municipal patriotism was one of the mainstays of
their hegemony. But wealth, legality, and respect for traditional authority notwithstanding, these men were outnumbered. Standing alone, the
moneyed class, the bourgeois men of property, would have been exposed
to subversion; they had to seek allies outside their class. They gained
many more allies during the sixteenth century than in earlier periods by
turning away from their origins.

Since the end of the Middle Ages, certain businessmen had ceased
participating in the political life of their city, an arena that they now
found too confining. If, in this century, some big merchants were still
pursuing municipal honors, others were obviously losing interest. The
center of attraction was no longer the city hall, but the Court. The
political decline of the cities took various forms. In Italy it appeared early
in the acceptance of the regime of the *signoria*. Despite the revolutionary upheavals that accompanied this development and which split the
business classes, the latter on the whole were not displeased by the
establishment of a tyrannical order that would hold the popular masses
in check. (Later on, foreign conquerors would perform this service.)
Elsewhere too, at a more or less rapid and abrupt pace, sovereigns were
rapidly extending their sway over the cities. The state was consolidating
its authority; the merchants who furnished the finances for its undertakings were beholden to it for the ratification of their power at the local
level or for strong support that bypassed the municipal authorities. This

new alliance was established at the expense of urban autonomy. Not that this autonomy vanished completely: Venice and some of the larger German cities maintained their independence. Even in the absolute monarchies of western Europe, the actual concentration of authority was not such that it could eradicate certain broad freedoms. Thus, in exchange for an obedience that rarely caused them any inconvenience, the bourgeois oligarchies were allowed to retain their most substantial privileges. Because of the international connections of the great merchant dynasties, sovereigns were compelled to show special consideration to these subjects, who, in fact, were often in a position to dictate (with due decorum) their own terms. Money was triumphant, but at the same time, the money interests were becoming enmeshed in a social sphere of which they were not really a part. This phenomenon had repercussions that went beyond the banker's fascination with Court.

At every level of the world of commerce, the same ambition was driving men to escape from the milieus where they had made their fortunes. The wealthiest entered the ranks of the upper aristocracy, while the others acquired—either directly or gradually, depending on their means—a less illustrious title of nobility. In most cases, becoming a landowner or purchasing an office (often both things were done at the same time) was the means by which the transition was effected. To explain this movement, it is not enough to cite the fantastic craving for titles and the desire for prestige, although these obviously were factors. A man's conception of the social hierarchy is inseparable from the interdependence of the social and economic structures. The class-climbing behavior of the bourgeoisie can be explained only by their weakness, and, of course, from a purely commercial point of view, the acquisition of land or offices was not always a bad investment. It was definitely advantageous for a merchant to have a son-in-law or brother-in-law serving as a councillor in the Parliament. Buying up properties, regrouping them, and exploiting them through a new system of land tenure (replacing permanent grants with tenant farming, for example) furthered the development of bourgeois-capitalist structures in the country-

Index

harper ✦ torchbooks

American Studies: General

HENRY STEELE COMMAGER, Ed.: The Struggle for Racial Equality TB/1300

CARL N. DEGLER: Out of Our Past: *The Forces that Shaped Modern America* CN/2

CARL N. DEGLER, Ed.: Pivotal Interpretations of American History
Vol. I TB/1240; Vol. II TB/1241

A. S. EISENSTADT, Ed.: The Craft of American History: *Selected Essays*
Vol. I TB/1255; Vol. II TB/1256

ROBERT L. HEILBRONER: The Limits of American Capitalism TB/1305

JOHN HIGHAM, Ed.: The Reconstruction of American History TB/1068

ROBERT H. JACKSON: The Supreme Court in the American System of Government TB/1106

JOHN F. KENNEDY: A Nation of immigrants. *Illus. Revised and Enlarged. Introduction by Robert F. Kennedy* TB/1118

RICHARD B. MORRIS: Fair Trial: *Fourteen Who Stood Accused, from Anne Hutchinson to Alger Hiss* TB/1335

GUNNAR MYRDAL: An American Dilemma: *The Negro Problem and Modern Democracy. Introduction by the Author.*
Vol. I TB/1443; Vol. II TB/1444

GILBERT OSOFSKY, Ed.: The Burden of Race: *A Documentary History of Negro-White Relations in America* TB/1405

ARNOLD ROSE: The Negro in America: *The Condensed Version of Gunnar Myrdal's* An American Dilemma. *Second Edition* TB/3048

JOHN E. SMITH: Themes in American Philosophy: *Purpose, Experience and Community* TB/1466

WILLIAM R. TAYLOR: Cavalier and Yankee: *The Old South and American National Character* TB/1474

American Studies: Colonial

BERNARD BAILYN: The New England Merchants in the Seventeenth Century TB/1149

ROBERT E. BROWN: Middle-Class Democracy and Revolution in Massachusetts, 1691–1780. *New Introduction by Author* TB/1413

JOSEPH CHARLES: The Origins of the American Party System TB/1049

WESLEY FRANK CRAVEN: The Colonies in Transition: 1660-1712† TB/3084

CHARLES GIBSON: Spain in America † TB/3077

CHARLES GIBSON, Ed.: The Spanish Tradition in America + HR/1351

LAWRENCE HENRY GIPSON: The Coming of the Revolution: 1763-1775. † *Illus.* TB/3007

PERRY MILLER: Errand Into the Wilderness TB/1139

PERRY MILLER & T. H. JOHNSON, Eds.: The Puritans: *A Sourcebook of Their Writings*
Vol. I TB/1093; Vol. II TB/1094

EDMUND S. MORGAN: The Puritan Family: *Religion and Domestic Relations in Seventeenth Century New England* TB/1227

WALLACE NOTESTEIN: The English People on the Eve of Colonization: 1603-1630. † *Illus.* TB/3006

LOUIS B. WRIGHT: The Cultural Life of the American Colonies: 1607-1763. † *Illus.* TB/3005

American Studies: The Revolution to 1860

JOHN R. ALDEN: The American Revolution: 1775-1783. † *Illus.* TB/3011

RAY A. BILLINGTON: The Far Western Frontier: 1830-1860. † *Illus.* TB/3012

GEORGE DANGERFIELD: The Awakening of American Nationalism, 1815-1828. † *Illus.* TB/3061

CLEMENT EATON: The Growth of Southern Civilization, 1790-1860. † *Illus.* TB/3040

LOUIS FILLER: The Crusade against Slavery: 1830-1860. † *Illus.* TB/3029

WILLIM W. FREEHLING: Prelude to Civil War: *The Nullification Controversy in South Carolina, 1816-1836* TB/1359

THOMAS JEFFERSON: Notes on the State of Virginia. ‡ *Edited by Thomas P. Abernethy* TB/3052

JOHN C. MILLER: The Federalist Era: 1789-1801. † *Illus.* TB/3027

RICHARD B. MORRIS: The American Revolution Reconsidered TB/1363

GILBERT OSOFSKY, Ed.: Puttin' On Ole Massa: *The Slave Narratives of Henry Bibb, William Wells Brown, and Solomon Northup* ‡ TB/1432

FRANCIS S. PHILBRICK: The Rise of the West, 1754-1830. † *Illus.* TB/3067

MARSHALL SMELSER: The Democratic Republic, 1801-1815 † TB/1406

† The New American Nation Series, edited by Henry Steele Commager and Richard B. Morris.
‡ American Perspectives series, edited by Bernard Wishy and William E. Leuchtenburg.
ᵃ History of Europe series, edited by J. H. Plumb.
§ The Library of Religion and Culture, edited by Benjamin Nelson.
‖ Researches in the Social, Cultural, and Behavioral Sciences, edited by Benjamin Nelson.
ᶻ Harper Modern Science Series, edited by James A. Newman.
° Not for sale in Canada.
+ Documentary History of the United States series, edited by Richard B. Morris.
# Documentary History of Western Civilization series, edited by Eugene C. Black and Leonard W. Levy.
ᴧ The Economic History of the United States series, edited by Henry David et al.
¶ European Perspectives series, edited by Eugene C. Black.
** Contemporary Essays series, edited by Leonard W. Levy.
* The Stratum Series, edited by John Hale.

LOUIS B. WRIGHT: Culture on the Moving Frontier TB/1053

American Studies: The Civil War to 1900

T. C. COCHRAN & WILLIAM MILLER: The Age of Enterprise: *A Social History of Industrial America* TB/1054
W. A. DUNNING: Reconstruction, Political and Economic: 1865-1877 TB/1073
HAROLD U. FAULKNER: Politics, Reform and Expansion: 1890-1900. † *Illus.* TB/3020
GEORGE M. FREDRICKSON: The Inner Civil War: *Northern Intellectuals and the Crisis of the Union* TB/1358
JOHN A. GARRATY: The New Commonwealth, 1877-1890 † TB/1410
HELEN HUNT JACKSON: A Century of Dishonor: *The Early Crusade for Indian Reform.* † *Edited by Andrew F. Rolle* TB/3063
WILLIAM G. MCLOUGHLIN, Ed.: The American Evangelicals, 1800-1900: An Anthology ‡ TB/1382
JAMES S. PIKE: The Prostrate State: *South Carolina under Negro Government.* ‡ *Intro. by Robert F. Durden* TB/3085
VERNON LANE WHARTON: The Negro in Mississippi, 1865-1890 TB/1178

American Studies: The Twentieth Century

RAY STANNARD BAKER: Following the Color Line: *American Negro Citizenship in Progressive Era.* ‡ *Edited by Dewey W. Grantham, Jr. Illus.* TB/3053
RANDOLPH S. BOURNE: War and the Intellectuals: *Collected Essays, 1915-1919.* ‡ *Edited by Carl Resek* TB/3043
A. RUSSELL BUCHANAN: The United States and World War II. † *Illus.*
Vol. I TB/3044; Vol. II TB/3045
THOMAS C. COCHRAN: The American Business System: *A Historical Perspective, 1900-1955* TB/1080
FOSTER RHEA DULLES: America's Rise to World Power: 1898-1954. † *Illus.* TB/3021
HAROLD U. FAULKNER: The Decline of Laissez Faire, 1897-1917 TB/1397
JOHN D. HICKS: Republican Ascendancy: 1921-1933. † *Illus.* TB/3041
WILLIAM E. LEUCHTENBURG: Franklin D. Roosevelt and the New Deal: 1932-1940. † *Illus.* TB/3025
WILLIAM E. LEUCHTENBURG, Ed.: The New Deal: *A Documentary History* + HR/1354
ARTHUR S. LINK: Woodrow Wilson and the Progressive Era: 1910-1917. † *Illus.* TB/3023
BROADUS MITCHELL: Depression Decade: *From New Era through New Deal, 1929-1941* ∧ TB/1439
GEORGE E. MOWRY: The Era of Theodore Roosevelt and the Birth of Modern America: 1900-1912. † *Illus.* TB/3022
WILLIAM PRESTON, JR.: Aliens and Dissenters: TWELVE SOUTHERNERS: I'll Take My Stand: *The South and the Agrarian Tradition. Intro. by Louis D. Rubin, Jr.; Biographical Essays by Virginia Rock* TB/1072

Art, Art History, Aesthetics

ERWIN PANOFSKY: Renaissance and Renascences in Western Art. *Illus.* TB/1447
ERWIN PANOFSKY: Studies in Iconology: *Humanistic Themes in the Art of the Renaissance. 180 illus.* TB/1077
HEINRICH ZIMMER: Myths and Symbols in Indian Art and Civilization. *70 illus.* TB/2005

Asian Studies

WOLFGANG FRANKE: China and the West: *The Cultural Encounter, 13th to 20th Centuries. Trans. by R. A. Wilson* TB/1326
L. CARRINGTON GOODRICH: A Short History of the Chinese People. *Illus.* TB/3015

Economics & Economic History

C. E. BLACK: The Dynamics of Modernization: *A Study in Comparative History* TB/1321
GILBERT BURCK & EDITORS OF *Fortune:* The Computer Age: *And its Potential for Management* TB/1179
ROBERT L. HEILBRONER: The Future as History: *The Historic Currents of Our Time and the Direction in Which They Are Taking America* TB/1386
ROBERT L. HEILBRONER: The Great Ascent: *The Struggle for Economic Development in Our Time* TB/3030
FRANK H. KNIGHT: The Economic Organization TB/1214
DAVID S. LANDES: Bankers and Pashas: *International Finance and Economic Imperialism in Egypt. New Preface by the Author* TB/1412
ROBERT LATOUCHE: The Birth of Western Economy: *Economic Aspects of the Dark Ages* TB/1290
W. ARTHUR LEWIS: The Principles of Economic Planning. *New Introduction by the Author°* TB/1436
WILLIAM MILLER, Ed.: Men in Business: *Essays on the Historical Role of the Entrepreneur* TB/1081
HERBERT A. SIMON: The Shape of Automation: *For Men and Management* TB/1245

Historiography and History of Ideas

J. BRONOWSKI & BRUCE MAZLISH: The Western Intellectual Tradition: *From Leonardo to Hegel* TB/3001
WILHELM DILTHEY: Pattern and Meaning in History: *Thoughts on History and Society.° Edited with an Intro. by H. P. Rickman* TB/1075
J. H. HEXTER: More's Utopia: *The Biography of an Idea. Epilogue by the Author* TB/1195
H. STUART HUGHES: History as Art and as Science: *Twin Vistas on the Past* TB/1207
ARTHUR O. LOVEJOY: The Great Chain of Being: *A Study of the History of an Idea* TB/1009
RICHARD H. POPKIN: The History of Scepticism from Erasmus to Descartes. *Revised Edition* TB/1391
BRUNO SNELL: The Discovery of the Mind: *The Greek Origins of European Thought* TB/1018

History: General

HANS KOHN: The Age of Nationalism: *The First Era of Global History* TB/1380
BERNARD LEWIS: The Arabs in History TB/1029
BERNARD LEWIS: The Middle East and the West ° TB/1274

History: Ancient

A. ANDREWS: The Greek Tyrants TB/1103
THEODOR H. GASTER: Thespis: *Ritual Myth and Drama in the Ancient Near East* TB/1281

A. H. M. JONES, Ed.: A History of Rome through the Fifth Century # *Vol. I: The Republic* HR/1364
Vol. II The Empire: HR/1460
SAMUEL NOAH KRAMER: Sumerian Mythology TB/1055
NAPHTALI LEWIS & MEYER REINHOLD, Eds.: Roman Civilization *Vol. I: The Republic* TB/1231
Vol. II: The Empire TB/1232

History: Medieval

NORMAN COHN: The Pursuit of the Millennium: *Revolutionary Messianism in Medieval and Reformation Europe* TB/1037
F. L. GANSHOF: Feudalism TB/1058
F. L. GANSHOF: The Middle Ages: *A History of International Relations. Translated by Rémy Hall* TB/1411
HENRY CHARLES LEA: The Inquisition of the Middle Ages. || *Introduction by Walter Ullmann* TB/1456

History: Renaissance & Reformation

JACOB BURCKHARDT: The Civilization of the Renaissance in Italy. *Introduction by Benjamin Nelson and Charles Trinkaus. Illus.* Vol. I TB/40; Vol. II TB/41
JOHN CALVIN & JACOPO SADOLETO: A Reformation Debate. *Edited by John C. Olin* TB/1239
J. H. ELLIOTT: Europe Divided, 1559-1598 a ° TB/1414
G. R. ELTON: Reformation Europe, 1517-1559 ° a TB/1270
HANS J. HILLERBRAND, Ed., The Protestant Reformation # HR/1342
JOHAN HUIZINGA: Erasmus and the Age of Reformation. *Illus.* TB/19
JOEL HURSTFIELD: The Elizabethan Nation TB/1312
JOEL HURSTFIELD, Ed.: The Reformation Crisis TB/1267
PAUL OSKAR KRISTELLER: Renaissance Thought: *The Classic, Scholastic, and Humanist Strains* TB/1048
DAVID LITTLE: Religion, Order and Law: *A Study in Pre-Revolutionary England.* § *Preface by R. Bellah* TB/1418
PAOLO ROSSI: Philosophy, Technology, and the Arts, in the Early Modern Era 1400-1700. || *Edited by Benjamin Nelson. Translated by Salvator Attanasio* TB/1458
H. R. TREVOR-ROPER: The European Witch-craze of the Sixteenth and Seventeenth Centuries and Other Essays ° TB/1416

History: Modern European

ALAN BULLOCK: Hitler, A Study in Tyranny. ° *Revised Edition. Illus.* TB/1123
JOHANN GOTTLIEB FICHTE: Addresses to the German Nation. *Ed. with Intro. by George A. Kelly* ¶ TB/1366
ALBERT GOODWIN: The French Revolution TB/1064
STANLEY HOFFMANN et al.: In Search of France: *The Economy, Society and Political System In the Twentieth Century* TB/1219
H. STUART HUGHES: The Obstructed Path: *French Social Thought in the Years of Desperation* TB/1451
JOHAN HUIZINGA: Dutch Civilisation in the 17th Century and Other Essays TB/1453

JOHN MCMANNERS: European History, 1789-1914: *Men, Machines and Freedom* TB/1419
HUGH SETON-WATSON: Eastern Europe Between the Wars, 1918-1941 TB/1330
ALBERT SOREL: Europe Under the Old Regime. *Translated by Francis H. Herrick* TB/1121
A. J. P. TAYLOR: From Napoleon to Lenin: *Historical Essays* ° TB/1268
A. J. P. TAYLOR: The Habsburg Monarchy, 1809-1918: *A History of the Austrian Empire and Austria-Hungary* ° TB/1187
J. M. THOMPSON: European History, 1494-1789 TB/1431
H. R. TREVOR-ROPER: Historical Essays TB/1269

Literature & Literary Criticism

W. J. BATE: From Classic to Romantic: *Premises of Taste in Eighteenth Century England* TB/1036
VAN WYCK BROOKS: Van Wyck Brooks: The Early Years: *A Selection from his Works, 1908-1921 Ed. with Intro. by Claire Sprague* TB/3082
RICHMOND LATTIMORE, Translator: The Odyssey of Homer TB/1389
ROBERT PREYER, Ed.: Victorian Literature ** TB/1302

Philosophy

HENRI BERGSON: Time and Free Will: *An Essay on the Immediate Data of Consciousness* ° TB/1021
H. J. BLACKHAM: Six Existentialist Thinkers: *Kierkegaard, Nietzsche, Jaspers, Marcel, Heidegger, Sartre* ° TB/1002
J. M. BOCHENSKI: The Methods of Contemporary Thought. *Trans. by Peter Caws* TB/1377
ERNST CASSIRER: Rousseau, Kant and Goethe. *Intro. by Peter Gay* TB/1092
MICHAEL GELVEN: A Commentary on Heidegger's "Being and Time" TB/1464
J. GLENN GRAY: Hegel and Greek Thought TB/1409
W. K. C. GUTHRIE: The Greek Philosophers: *From Thales to Aristotle* ° TB/1008
G. W. F. HEGEL: Phenomenology of Mind. ° || *Introduction by George Lichtheim* TB/1303
MARTIN HEIDEGGER: Discourse on Thinking. *Translated with a Preface by John M. Anderson and E. Hans Freund. Introduction by John M. Anderson* TB/1459
F. H. HEINEMANN: Existentialism and the Modern Predicament TB/28
WERER HEISENBERG: Physics and Philosophy: *The Revolution in Modern Science. Intro. by F. S. C. Northrop* TB/549
EDMUND HUSSERL: Phenomenology and the Crisis of Philosophy. § *Translated with an Introduction by Quentin Lauer* TB/1170
IMMANUEL KANT: Groundwork of the Metaphysic of Morals. *Translated and Analyzed by H. J. Paton* TB/1159
WALTER KAUFMANN, Ed.: Religion From Tolstoy to Camus: *Basic Writings on Religious Truth and Morals* TB/123
QUENTIN LAUER: Phenomenology: *Its Genesis and Prospect. Preface by Aron Gurwitsch* TB/1169
MICHAEL POLANYI: Personal Knowledge: *Towards a Post-Critical Philosophy* TB/1158
WILLARD VAN ORMAN QUINE: Elementary Logic *Revised Edition* TB/577
WILHELM WINDELBAND: A History of Philosophy *Vol. I: Greek, Roman, Medieval* TB/38

4